2/20/16

Tiff —

You are such a blessing. It was such an honor to watch the hands of God's healing at work in your life tonight! This book will truly bless you!

Donna Adams

Wound Care: Healing from the Inside Out

Wound Care: Healing from the Inside Out

Dana Adams

Copyright © 2015 by Dana Adams.

Library of Congress Control Number:		2015920339
ISBN:	Hardcover	978-1-5144-3331-7
	Softcover	978-1-5144-3330-0
	eBook	978-1-5144-3329-4

All rights reserved. No part of this book may be reproduced or transmitted in any form or by any means, electronic or mechanical, including photocopying, recording, or by any information storage and retrieval system, without permission in writing from the copyright owner.

Scripture quotations marked NKJV are taken from the New King James Version. © 1982 by *Thomas Nelson Inc*. Used by permission. All rights reserved.

Scripture quotations marked MSG are taken from The Message. © 1993, 1994, 1995, 1996, 2000, 2001, 2002, 2003 by Eugene H. Peterson. Used by permission of *NavPress* Publishing Group. *Website*.

Any people depicted in stock imagery provided by Thinkstock are models, and such images are being used for illustrative purposes only. Certain stock imagery © Thinkstock.

Print information available on the last page.

Rev. date: 12/10/2015

To order additional copies of this book, contact:
Xlibris
1-888-795-4274
www.Xlibris.com
Orders@Xlibris.com
727523

Contents

Preface xi

Introduction xv

PART 1
How Wounds Infect You and Others

Chapter 1   The Birth of the First Wound 3
Chapter 2   Shame Turns to Blame 7
Chapter 3   Wounded to Win 11

PART 2
The Stages of Healing

Chapter 4   The Wound Has to Be Addressed 17
Chapter 5   The Wound Has to Be Exposed 23
Chapter 6   Tears Lubricate the Wound 27
Chapter 7   It Gets Messy before It Gets Better 33

PART 3
The Wound Care Kit

Chapter 8   The Wound Care Kit: Praise 51
Chapter 9   The Wound Care Kit: Prayer 56
Chapter 10   The Wound Care Kit: People 68
Chapter 11   The Wound Care Kit: Bible 74

PART 4
Staying Healed

Chapter 12 Shake It Off 85
Chapter 13 Speak to Your Mountain 88
Chapter 14 Staying Healed Is Serving a Greater Vision 97
Chapter 15 Staying Healed Is Having Next-Generation Generosity 107
Conclusion 115

But He was wounded for our transgressions, He was bruised for our iniquities; The chastisement for our peace was upon Him, And by His stripes we are healed.

—Isaiah 53:5 (NKJV)

To all who read this book, let me encourage you with a prayer straight from the Word of God:

> I ask that you may be filled with the knowledge of His will in all wisdom and spiritual understanding; that you may walk worthy of the Lord, fully pleasing Him, being fruitful in every good work and increasing in the knowledge of God; strengthened with all might, according to His glorious power, for all patience and longsuffering with joy; giving thanks to the Father who has qualified us to be partakers of the inheritance of the saints in the light.
>
> —Colossians 1:9 (NKJV)

Preface

As an ICU nurse practicing for nearly twelve years, it has become very clear to me that there has never been a greater time where we are dealing with more signs and symptoms of unaddressed pain versus people. When pain and wounds are not properly dealt with, the person can no longer repress the pain. They begin to manifest physically because they can no longer hide their issues. Our hospital beds are full of people desperately crying out for help, solutions, and resolve. Unfortunately, in the health-care world, we find it much easier to slap a diagnosis on a person, treat that diagnosis, and send them on their way, never addressing the person or the root issue: wounds unaddressed.

I work in an environment that places emphasis on symptom management. In reality, I don't agree with this approach, but my mission is to always care for the person, not the symptom. While caring for my patients requires short-term care of their physical needs, my aim is always to find out their story. The issue is not the disease process; the issue is the underlying root, which is causing the condition. When we begin to see the physical manifestations, we are seeing the most extreme forms of wounds unaddressed. You can hide anger, bitterness, resentment, unforgiveness, and animosity, but you can't hide cancer, heart disease, stroke, autoimmune disease, inflammatory disease, depression, addiction, or the unexplained illness. Eventually, those deep-rooted issues can no longer hide beneath the surface.

When a patient comes in with a massive head bleed from using crystal meth, we often fix the head bleed through an intervention, rehabilitate them, and discharge them. Then they are readmitted to an ER the very same day, seeking drugs to ease pain and anxiety. Why? Because the Western medicine world culture focuses on diagnosing and treating the symptom to avoid the difficult conversation. With health-care reform, roles have been restructured with an emphasis on the paperwork, so a patient becomes more of a billing code than a person. Would things be different if we took more time to get down to the root of the problem causing the condition in the first place? When I was initially called to the nursing profession, I truly did love people, and this approach of health care seemed normal to me. It wasn't until I became aware of my own wounds and unprocessed pain that my paradigms shifted. After God radically healed me from the inside out, I now know that I was called to work in an environment that I don't necessarily agree with—not to be conformed to it but to transform it.

As health-care professionals, we are often deceived, and we do not deal with our own messes because we numb ourselves by caring for people who seem worse off than us. In reality, we are actually the victims of the same generational oppression, relational brokenness, isolation, and bondage.

I was once one of those victims. I would hide my own issues because I was deceived to believe my problems weren't nearly as bad as one fighting for life, but I was losing the battle.

Eventually, it all came to the surface, and I went through a life-changing healing process. Now I truly do love caring for people and have more compassion and empathy than ever before. I've created more space in my heart by getting rid of old patterns of behavior and toxic thinking. I now have a greater capacity to love others.

With the love and the experiences that have been so integral to my healing process, I have a responsibility now to share my story and wisdom gained in that process to help restore the afflicted, broken, and wounded. Whether I'm a nurse at the bedside, ministering to someone on an altar at church on Sunday, or meeting someone to counsel in a coffee shop, I see my former self in these people. Their circumstances may be different, but the issues are the same. Their root issues are so easy to discern because I've been where they are on the journey. I now have grounds and authority to speak to these issues and disciple others on the road to healing and recovery.

As I was praying for more career opportunities, God spoke to me about this book. I had wanted to earn more money without working overtime in the ICU because of the physical demands and stress. I was asking God to give me dreams, visions, and new ideas. I wanted to do something radical and something other people weren't doing.

Randomly, I was at work one day filling up my water bottle in the break area, and the Holy Spirit spoke to me and clearly said, "If you want the revenue, write the book."

It was then I knew I was on assignment. This book is truly an act of obedience and inspired by none other than the Holy Spirit. I have done the work but can't take the credit. To God be all the glory.

We were created to have dominion, to have all wisdom, knowledge, and understanding through a process.

This book was written to help people in one or more of three categories: those who do not recognize they have not dealt with their wounds (or have no understanding of the role their undealt wounds play in every area of their lives); those who know they have undealt wounds causing a detrimental struggle, but they don't know how or are frightened to go through the healing process; or those who have become aware of the wounds and gone through the healing process but don't know that staying healed is a lifetime process; they do not understand that the biggest battles they will face from this point on are the battles to stay healed.

As I was undergoing this process in my life, the Lord gave me a vision one day as I was taking care of a patient's deeply infected physical wound at the bedside. Interestingly enough, I was in an isolation room. Isolation rooms are for patients with infections highly resistant to antibiotics. These patients are so contagious that the infection becomes a threat to them and other people. Anyone coming in close contact with these patients must wear personal protective equipment so that they are not contaminated and, in return, do not contaminate others.

As I was removing the bandage from the deeply infected wound and exposing it, I heard the still small voice of God ask me, "Dana, you are a nurse, right?"

I replied, "Yes, God, of course, I am."

He said again, "Well, don't you know that a wound has to be healed from the inside out?" It was then I realized that God addresses wounds in the spirit just as we do as nurses at the bedside in the natural. He began to show me each part of the healing process through revealing those processes to me in the context of His Word. Instantly, I understood the outcomes of wounds not properly addressed and treated. When we don't deal with our wounds, when we keep putting Band-Aids on and treating the symptoms versus exposing the root, our wounds open up to infections, and we infect others.

God is our ultimate healer, and He created us to live from a place of freedom. By His stripes, we have been healed, we are being healed, and we will be healed. If we fail to stay the course, we won't stay healed; we were designed to stay the course!

This book will take you on a journey through the course of my life and how I was healed from the inside out, but more importantly, it will point you to the Word of God and what He says about these areas. As long as we walk this earth, we will be in a process, and healing is a process! No matter where you are on the journey, come along, be encouraged, be transformed, experience genuine healing as the Lord your God intended, and be forever changed!

Introduction

In 2010, I started going to C3 Church San Diego. I was a mess on legs. I had all my preconceived ways of thinking, mind-sets, and habits. I decided to call this church my home. Immediately, I wanted to get planted and start serving. What I loved about this church was that it didn't elevate gifting; it elevated character with the understanding that gifting only takes you so far, but character lasts a lifetime. Naturally, I leaned toward leading worship because that is what I had always done at previous churches. I joined the worship team, but I wasn't promoted immediately. I wasn't given a platform to worship lead. In fact, it was a long time before I could lead a song. There actually needed to be some character development; God had to shift some mind-sets, so it wasn't me getting the glory but Him.

They started asking me to do some things outside of my comfort zone. I remember being on a jog, and I was crying out to the Lord, "Why are you doing this to me? I'm not qualified! There are people way more qualified to do this! Why me?" I clearly heard the Holy Spirit say, "Dana, I didn't choose them. I chose you. Dana, your capacity is limited by your unavailability in your heart."

I let that word resonate for quite some time because at that time, I didn't understand what God was saying, but I did make a choice. I chose to turn my "whys" into "whats." I chose to take on the tasks that I had been given and to start serving in an uncomfortable place.

It was a really messy process, and it still is at times. I began to feel pressure; it was like God was really beginning to turn up the heat in my life. Sometimes God has to turn up the heat in our world because there is only one way to refine us so that we can do what it is He has called us to do.

God began to speak to me in a series of prophetic dreams. I remember one where we were in our first church building, a gym in a boys and girls club. I was sitting in the front row, and I remember looking up to see all of the worship leaders from my childhood.

The worship was incredible! I was engaged, lifting my hands, when all of a sudden a little girl appeared at my feet with a pail of water and said, "I have a word for you. Can I wash your feet?" I looked at her like she had two heads and exclaimed, "Do you have to do this now? I am trying to worship here. Can't we do this another time?" But I remembered she was so persistent! Worship ended, and my pastor got up to start preaching. I remember him looking at the little girl in this dream and taking note of what she was doing as he continued preaching.

Finally, I gave in and said, "Okay, if you must do this, we need to move to another more discrete area! We moved, and she came over with her pail of water. I remember how meticulous she was with my feet. As she took such incredible care of my feet, she looked up at me and said, "I have a word for you. You were meant to have boldness." The dream ended.

The next morning, I woke up asking God what the dream was all about. I knew I was called to leadership, but was He telling me I needed to wash my people's feet? I didn't understand . . . and then it dawned on me . . . the little girl in the dream was me.

This was a very prophetic dream. I didn't recognize the little girl in the dream because she had dark hair. As a child, I had blond hair, but at that time, my hair was dark. God was speaking to me, through me, about me.

That little girl loved the presence of God and resting in Him. The Holy Spirit spoke to me and said, "Dana, there is nothing that I have called you to where I will not bathe you in grace, but you need to understand, to go there, you have to go back to her."

Even though I was that girl that loved being in the presence of God, I got caught up in the busyness and the cares of life—the present, still Mary had become a worried, anxious Martha.

Sometimes, we do have to go back. We don't want to dwell in the past, but sometimes we have to go back to deal with the things that keep us from seeing our future. Your past does not dictate your future. When we go back and deal with these things, we can move forward and do what it is that God has called us to do.

We struggle with issues not only such as these but also addictions, depression, unexplained illness, and other bondages. We are deceived to believe that we were patterned or born this way. We believe it is our fault that we are in certain situations.

The truth is God is a God of healing and restoration. He wants to restore us back to the place we were destined to be. When we are put back into connection with who God is, we can see who we are. The greater image of God that we get on the inside of us, the greater perspective we have for what we are called to be.

Jeremiah 1:5 (NKJV) says, "Before I formed you in the womb I knew you; Before you were born I sanctified you." This is your God-given reality! A God-given reality cannot agree with bondage, addiction, depression, or unexplained illness. These were not predestined patterns of behavior, but they are patterns of behavior that began a long time ago and have never been dealt with from generation to generation.

In the first section of this book, we are going to travel back to where it all began because we need to unpackage the lie so the truth can be revealed. We are going to travel back to the Garden of Eden, the birth of the first wound.

Part 1

How Wounds Infect You and Others

Chapter 1

The Birth of the First Wound

God created us to be in relationship, not isolation.

Genesis 3:1–6 (NKJV) says, "Now the serpent was more cunning than any beast of the field which the Lord God has made. And he said to the woman, 'Has God indeed said, You shall not eat of every tree of the garden?' And the woman said to the serpent, 'We may eat the fruit of the trees of the garden; but of the fruit of the tree which is in the midst of the garden, God has said, You shall not eat it, nor shall you touch it, lest you die.' Then the serpent said to the woman, 'You will not surely die. For God knows that in the day you eat of it your eyes will be opened, and you will be like God, knowing good and evil.' So when the woman saw that the tree was good for food, that it was pleasant to the eyes, and a tree desirable to make one wise, she took of its fruit and ate."

Every year, I do a one-year chronological study of the Bible, and I often get stuck in the book of Genesis. This year, when I came across this passage of scripture, God showed me something new.

He showed me that the serpent was called cunning for a good reason. Before the serpent deceived Eve, he isolated her. He found her weak, vulnerable, and in a compromised state. There was no one around to see him approaching or to help her. As a result, he was easily able to deceive her.

Deception means partial truth. If he could appeal to the good side, the immediate gratification, she would see the fruit as desirable, and she would partake. She didn't even know she was being deceived. If she knew she was being deceived, it wouldn't be called deception.

She took the fruit and ate, but she didn't see what was on the other side of it; she didn't see that her choice would impact generations. It was actually the birth of the first wound, deception, which continues to be the devil's playground. If he can deceive us through isolation, he has us exactly where he wants us.

It was here that the devil employed another great tactic, a tactic he used then and continues to use today. If he could get her isolated and deceive her, then he could contradict the Word of God by getting her to question it. What did he say in Genesis 3:1 (NKJV)? "Has God indeed said you shall not eat of every tree of the garden?"

If he could use something as small as a fruit to deceive Eve, what can he use for us when we are in a weakened and compromised state? Where is that area for us in a place of isolation? What are the promises God has given that Satan tries to steal and contradict in that isolated place?

Did God really say He would save our loved ones? Did God really say He would heal us from that unexplained illness? Did God really say He would provide for us if we tithed in His house? Did God really say He would bring us a spouse?

We can see how these patterns begin. In the isolated place, the place of deception, Eve, like many of us, chose to believe what was in the space between her right and her left ear versus what the Word of God said. She was in a place of compromise.

Compromise doesn't begin overnight; people don't just go out and start ruining their lives. Compromise begins in our mind. I often wonder if things would have been different if Adam would have been there with her. She was unprotected, uncovered, and there was no one to tell her danger was approaching.

I saw this in my own life. I can understand Eve's position. When asked to start overseeing the local missions area at my church, I had put all the work in building from the foundation up and then moved on to start bringing in the people and building teams.

One morning, I was in prayer at 5:00 a.m., and I was asking God to teach me how to be a disciple, to see the gold in people, and to reproduce myself. I was in the midst of praying very passionately when I heard the Holy Spirit say, "There are some things that don't need to be reproduced."

I was shocked! How could He speak to me like this when I had carved out thirty minutes of my precious beauty sleep to get up and pray! I couldn't even believe He was talking to me like that. But the Holy Spirit knew that the Martha struggle was real, so 5:00 a.m. was the only time He could get my attention!

After He spoke to me, He really didn't say anything else, but God often says a lot in His silence.

Instead, He began to speak through other people. I would be out at church functions, and some of the members on my team would truthfully say, "Dana, you are a little on the task-heavy side. You are not very approachable." I started to hear it more often and didn't really get it until I was out at breakfast with a good friend of mine. He happened to be a guy. We were speaking about dating. I wasn't exactly being very positive, and the guy laughed at me and said, "Dana, if I was a guy in the church, I wouldn't even approach you."

Wow! I think I felt a little chest pain, shortness of breath, and dizziness! Even though it was hard, I knew what he said was right. I told him so and that I was going to do something about it.

I was praying again, much more humble this time, and I told God, "Lord, I know what he said was true, but what is true about it?" He said, "Dana, I want you to look to your right and to your left and tell Me what you see." I thought about it, and I had to admit that for a long time, I didn't see anyone. There was no one to the right and to the left of me. He said, "See, and don't think that just because you are in a room full of people means that you are not isolated." I had become so heavenly minded that I had no earthly sense! I had become so task-heavy that I lost the importance of relationships.

It was then He gave me Ecclesiastes 4:7(MSG):

> "I turned my head and saw yet another wisp of smoke on its way to nothingness: a solitary person, completely alone-no children, no family, no friends—yet working obsessively late into the night, compulsively greedy for more and more, never bothering to ask, 'why am I working like a dog, never having any fun?' And who cares? More smoke. A bad business. It's better to have a partner than to go it alone. Share the work, share the wealth. And if one falls down, the other helps, But if there's no one to help, tough! Two in a bed warm each other. Alone, you shiver all night. By yourself you're unprotected. With a friend you can

face the worst. Can you round up a third? A three-stranded rope isn't easily snapped."

Sometimes, in ministry life, we are trying to point people to God, but sometimes, God is actually trying to point us back to people. We need people to do life with us.

Phil Pringle, founder of C3 Churches worldwide, once made this very powerful statement. He says, "Ninety percent of God's call on your life is in other people." We need people to see our blind spots, but they also win with us. People step out with us, take territory with us, and help us when we are down. There are people that come alongside of us to keep the promises alive when the circumstances of life don't measure up. When our faith is diminished, people help renew the promises.

Chapter 2

Shame Turns to Blame

Genesis 2:18 (NKJV) says, "And the Lord God said, 'It is not good that man should be alone; I will make him a helper comparable to him.' Out of the ground the Lord formed every beast of the field and every bird of the air, and brought to them to Adam to see what he would call them. And whatever Adam called each living creature, that was its name. So Adam gave names to all cattle, birds of the air, and to every beast of the field. But for Adam there was not found a helper comparable to him. And the Lord God caused a deep sleep to fall on Adam, and he slept; and He took one of his ribs, and closed up the flesh in its place. Then the rib which the Lord had taken from man, he made into woman, and He brought her to the man. And Adam said: 'This is now bone of my bones and flesh of my flesh; She shall be called Woman, because she was taken out of Man.' Therefore, a man shall leave his father and mother and be joined to his wife, and they shall become one flesh. And they were both naked, the man and his wife and were not ashamed."

Now let's pick up from where we left off in Genesis 3:6 (NKJV) after Eve was tempted with the fruit from the Tree of the Knowledge of Good and Evil and eats.

"So when the woman saw that the tree was good for food, that it was pleasant to the eyes, and a tree desirable to make one wise, she took of its fruit and ate. She also gave to her husband with her and he ate. Then the eyes of both of them were opened, and they knew that they were naked;

and they sewed fig leaves together and made themselves coverings. And they heard the sound of the Lord walking in the garden in the cool of the day, and Adam and his wife hid themselves from the presence of the Lord God among the trees of the garden. Then the Lord God called to Adam and said to him, 'Where are you?' So he said, 'I heard your voice in the garden, and I was afraid because I was naked; and I hid myself.' And he said, 'Who told you that you were naked? Have you eaten from the tree of which I have commanded that you should not eat?'"

Before this all happened, God created two perfect people who were living in a perfect place. Now they were being deceived. Two people who were created to work with one another were now working against one another. Deception wouldn't be as powerful if it didn't invite a few friends because we know that misery loves company. Eve introduces the lie to her husband, and he buys it. The wound of deception opened up into an infection and now continues to be an epidemic from generation to generation.

The Bible says that eyes of Adam and Eve were opened, and they knew both good and evil. Essentially, they became wise in their own eyes. Instead of being naïve, transparent, and unashamed, they realized they were no longer perfect. In their shame, they began to hide themselves from the presence of God by covering themselves up with fig leaves. Their naivety was replaced with fear and shame in the form of hard coverings, fig leaves.

God called out to them in the heat of the day in his mercy, but in their fear and shame, they hid from His presence. What happens next? Shame turns to blame. Like many of us, Adam and Eve began to carry shame. We shame ourselves and, in return, shame other people. We see it so clearly as the story continues.

Genesis 3:12–13 (NKJV) says, "Then the man said, 'The woman whom you gave to be with me, she gave me of the tree and I ate.' (This is where the battle of the sexes begins!) And the Lord God said to the woman, 'What is this you have done?' The woman said, 'The serpent deceived me, and I ate.'"

I saw a similar pattern in my own life. I started noticing negative patterns of behavior in my life. I wanted so desperately to break these cycles. I was so tired of going through the same old things!

I needed a complete surrender of my life to break the habitual cycles, so I joined the internship at my church. The internship program was designed to address any restraint keeping you from fulfilling the call of God on your life. Often, the cyclic patterns of behavior are broken in this process!

Prior to beginning this internship, I had a prophetic dream.

The dream began with an eye-fluttering open, and I could see myself on a stage, leading worship. When I looked out to the congregation, I saw demonic spirits hovering over people's heads. The Holy Spirit was speaking to me, saying, "Dana, I want you to look out and interpret what is happening in the spiritual climate and minister to it not just by your voice but by your body language. To effectively minister, I need you to understand something."

He took me to another room where I saw people on their knees in worship and the hand of God was moving through them. He had an egg in His hand, which was a bit strange. As He passed by each person, He would crack the egg, and the yoke would pour down on their faces. He would say, "I'm breaking this!" He would move onto the next person and say, "I'm breaking this, I'm breaking this, and I'm breaking this!" He took me back to the scene where I was leading worship and said, "I want you to interpret what is happening and minister to it, but you have to understand one thing. The yoke is not just upon you (like the people who were in the room who had taken on the burdens of the people they were ministering to)—the yoke is within you."

I immediately woke up in a state of alarm and realized that the Holy Spirit had just showed me my oppression! In the wee hours of the morning, I began to pray, cast, and break off fear, shame, doubt, and condemnation—everything I could think of in that moment!

I finally fell back to sleep and awoke the next morning. The dream was still so alive and real! It was such a prophetic, profound dream! I began praying, asking God for a deeper revelation of the dream; I did a word search on yoke.

To my amazement, I found that there are yoke muscles in your eyes. This was a crazy finding! At that time, I had been a nurse for almost nine years. I took anatomy and physiology but had never learned of yoke muscles in the eye! How good is God? He is always showing us something new! Yoke muscles determine where you fix your gaze.

In the dream, I was looking through the eyes of Jesus. I could see myself the way that He saw me. The Holy Spirit showed me that up until that point, I was being deceived and thought I was serving other people, but I was actually very self-focused. God was trying so desperately to

9

show me how He could see me, but I couldn't fully see it because I was so entangled in bondage.

When the Holy Spirit showed this to me, I immediately surrendered and put the cards on the table. I said, "God, I am going to let You reveal all of this stuff to me." And the Holy Spirit spoke again and said, "Dana, the issue is numbness. You are going to have to let the coverings—the guilt, the shame, the condemnation, the fig—leaves go away, and you are going to have to let pain take its course."

For the next year, I went through an intense grieving process. During that year, I realized that from the time I was a small child, I faced disappointment, discouragement, and failure, but I had put coping mechanisms into place not to feel these emotions.

The next thirty-plus years, I stayed numb. Now I actually had to face the numbness with no filter and let pain take its course. God was so faithful that He fully lifted the veil. He exposed everything that was hiding me from His presence, from knowing His ways, and from living life free and unashamed. I was able to break the cycles of victim mentality and repeated patterns of behavior that had been manifesting themselves in my life. I had been living according to who I thought I was versus the woman God uniquely created for greatness.

Fully exposed with no fig leaves, God was able to transform me! Now I can really see His hand at work in my life. What I have come to understand is that God wants to transform us, but we must allow Him to see us.

Chapter 3

Wounded to Win

Genesis 1:26 (NKJV) says, "Then God said, let us make human beings in our image, according to Our likeness; Let them have dominion over the fish of the sea, over the birds of the air, and over the cattle, over the earth and over every creeping thing that creeps on the earth. So God created man in his own image; in the image of God he created him; male and female He created them. Then God blessed them, and God said to them, 'Be fruitful and multiply; fill the Earth and subdue it; have dominion over the fish of the sea, over the birds of the air, and over every living thing that moves on the earth.'"

We were created for a life of abundance—a life of not just enough but more than enough. You were created to be a blessing so that you can bless other people. Even before the fall of man in the garden, God had already blessed us; His Word can't return to Him void. Somehow, we live like we are under a curse because deceptive patterns of behavior over time have led us to believe this about ourselves! On the other hand, if we take a closer look at the text, God never cursed us; He cursed the serpent and then He cursed the ground.

Genesis 3:14 (NKJV) says, "So the Lord God said to the serpent: 'Because you have done this, you are cursed more than all cattle, And more than every beast of the field; On your belly you shall go. And you shall eat dust all the days of your life.'"

We aren't cursed because we have already been blessed! Further down, he showed me another thing.

In Genesis 3:16 (NKJV), it says, "To the woman he said: 'I will greatly multiply your sorrow and your conception; In pain you shall bring forth children; Your desire shall be for your husband, And he shall rule over you.'"

What God showed me is that even a life of blessing has its challenges. The things that cause us the most pain will often bring us the most joy. Even children can bring joy, but they can also cause the most pain.

Sometimes the battle is over the blessing, and sometimes you have to overcome the challenges in order for that blessing to come to fruition. But this is my favorite part! Here in Genesis, we see that God in His mercy has a redemption plan!

In Genesis 3 (NKJV), God is talking to the serpent: "And I will put enmity Between you and the woman, And between your seed and her Seed; He shall bruise your head, And you shall bruise His heel."

See, this was actually a prophetic word of a coming Messiah! The redemption plan actually came through a human! We weren't created to be a problem; we were actually created to be part of the solution! Jesus would go to the cross. He would be crucified and pay the price for all of our guilt, shame, fear, and condemnation. His heel would be bruised, but in three days, He would be resurrected and crush the head of Satan! Jesus already did it all! Satan was defeated over two thousand years ago! Jesus already did it, but He created you and me to reverse the curse!

What the devil meant for evil God meant for good, and He does that through bringing people into a relationship with Him and into relationships with people!

We serve a God who knows the beginning from the end! He created us for good, not harm! He created us with the intention that we would come into a relationship with Him and live in blessing. However, man sins, and one act destroys His intentions! This destruction resulted in toxic patterns of behavior that have never been addressed from generation to generation.

We have to address these issues if we want to walk out the call of God on our lives. Every single one of us was created with a purpose and a destiny on the inside of us. In addition, it is this generation's responsibility not to let the yoke of oppression seep into the next generation.

It is time to turn that deception into reception! What curse have you been dealing with? Maybe it is sickness, lack, depression, oppression, addictions, broken marriages, or broken relationships. It's time to stop being conformed to our circumstances and what the world says about us and to be transformed by what the Word of God says. Today is your day for breakthrough!

Even before you were formed in your mother's womb, He knew you! Even while you were a sinner, He chose you! Circumstances fail, but His Word remains. He will never leave you or forsake you!

Part 2

The Stages of Healing

Chapter 4

The Wound Has to Be Addressed

Now we know that wounds have been around for quite a long time! Even as far back as the Old Testament, wounds unaddressed were considered to be very serious, in need of being addressed and tended to, or they became highly infectious!

Let's look at Leviticus 13 (MSG) at the laws concerning leprosy. It says, "God spoke to Moses and Aaron: 'When someone has a swelling or a blister or a shiny spot on the skin that might signal a serious skin disease on the body, bring him to Aaron the priest or to one of his priest sons. The priest will examine the sore on the skin. If the hair in the sore has turned white and the sore appears more than skin deep, it is a serious skin disease and infectious. After the priest has examined it, he will pronounce the person unclean.'"

The entire chapter is dedicated to serious skin conditions! It further goes into detail about swelling, scabs, and bright spots. Even though these were all minor ailments, the victims of the serious skin conditions were examined by the priest, pronounced unclean, quarantined (or isolated from others), until they brought no further concern. For some, it was only a few days, and others for an extended period of time.

The NKJV Study Bible Commentary actually discusses that the most serious result of the priest's examination was to be declared unclean and banished from the camp. In addition, it was the natural tendency of people to put off seeing the priest about a condition because of fear of that very declaration! Ritual uncleanness was a serious matter for all of the people. It was important to diagnose skin problems immediately so that the whole camp did not become unclean. If the afflicted person did not come on his own initiative, his family and clan leaders were responsible for bringing him. The priest would examine and make the diagnosis, but nothing was said about how to treat the ailments![1] The passage doesn't focus on the medical treatment but the ritual impurity and ensuring that community would not become unclean. Leprosy in those days was highly contagious and hereditary.

What an interesting correlation! This sounds like the scenario I previously described at the bedside with my infected patient! It's interesting that wounds have always been an immediate issue needing to be addressed, given immediate attention to keep from further infecting not just the person contaminated but the people around them. On the other hand, no one had the real answers for treating the condition! The priests were only able to declare a person leprous or infectious, focus on the state of impurity, and force the person into isolation. It's interesting to note that the people were so shamed by their infected state, they would avoid going to the priest, much like people today keep themselves covered to avoid exposing the wound and dealing with the painful process!

I'm so thankful that with the crucifixion and resurrection of Jesus Christ, we don't have to address wounds through the filter of judgment and condemnation! Jesus gave his life so that we don't just diagnose and treat symptoms, giving people names they were never meant to have, but we now have the answer for how to treat the ailments. We can now address the serious, diseased states through a filter of grace, which always addresses the person, not the problem.

Before Jesus, we had no real solution, but His ministry and the life He gave changed everything. Through the Holy Spirit, people are now empowered to address the wound and not just begin the healing process but also complete it to the finish!

Unfortunately, if one is without the full understanding of grace and does not have a relationship with Christ, they tend to see themselves as a serious problem, they live their lives based out of the identity of their problem, and they become a serious problem to others!

---

[1] Radmacher, Earl D., Ronald B. Allen, and H. Wayne House, eds. *NKJV Study Bible*. Tennessee: Thomas Nelson, 1982.

Now let's look at the New Testament approach and how it greatly contrasts the former approach. The key ingredient is Jesus; He has a way of shifting everything!

Let's look at John 5 (NKJV) and the way Jesus healed the paralytic man.

First of all, Jesus was not afraid to break the traditions of Jewish Law, which said that you could not heal on the Sabbath. This proves that healing is not ever convenient. Jesus wasn't into laws and traditions; He was into people. He would go to extraordinary lengths, taking the necessary time to ensure healing happened.

John 5 (NKJV) says, "After this there was a feast of the Jews, and Jesus went up to Jerusalem. Now there is in Jerusalem by the Sheep Gate a pool, which is called in Hebrew, Bethesda, having five porches. In these lay a great multitude of sick people, blind, lame, paralyzed, waiting for the moving of the water. For an angel went down at a certain time into the pool and stirred up the water; then whoever stepped in first, after the stirring of the water, was made well of whatever disease he had.

"Now a certain man was there who had an infirmity thirty-eight years. When Jesus saw him lying there, and knew that he already had been in that condition a long time, He said to him, 'Do you want to be made well?' The sick man answered Him, 'Sir, I have no man to put me into the pool when the water is stirred up; but while I am coming, another steps down before me.' Jesus said to him, 'Rise, take up your bed and walk.' And immediately the man was made well, took up his bed, and walked."

Let's stop right there. It's interesting that this man had a lingering disorder, but the disorder was not actually the issue; the issue was his victim mentality, a deep-"rooted" issue. Jesus couldn't deal with the man until he dealt with the root! This man had been missing out on his miracle for thirty-eight years, watching, while others stepped ahead of him and got their miracles, as he remained there helpless.

Watch what Jesus does! Jesus doesn't call the man a paralytic or talk about the physical manifestations of the condition. Instead, He challenges him with a question. "Do you want to get well?" This led to the man's confession that indeed he did want to get well! Jesus did not stretch His hand toward the paralytic man and command that he be healed. Instead, Jesus said, "Get up! Pick up your sleeping pad and walk!" Jesus basically said, "I am not going to do it for you, take responsibility for your healing!" Instantly (once he took action and moved), the man was healed! He became well, recovered his strength, picked up his bed, and walked! It was not until the man got up out of his victimized, idle state, and took his mat in obedience to Jesus's command that he was actually healed! This man was radically healed when he participated in his own miracle!

A thirty-eight-year helpless struggle turned into a miracle when the man stopped waiting for help and moved in response to the helper! In an instant, he was transformed from victim to victor! This was only possible because Jesus addressed the wound. However, He didn't address the wound by calling the person the disease or the problem. Instead, He addressed it by empowering him to move toward the miracle! He taught us that while it is important to address problems, issues, and wounds, it is even more important to know how to properly address them! He addressed the wound then, and even now, through the motivation of unconditional love.

Although it is not our might and not our power but by His Spirit we can do anything, we have to initiate this process! We have to take part in our own miracle! We have to stop waiting for God to move in our health, relationships, and finances; we have to make the first move! Yes, the Bible says we can do nothing set apart from God, but with God, all things are possible! You never make that move alone! The Lord is with you every step of the way!

Jesus himself demonstrated this example by doing what He saw His Father do. In doing so, He led others to do what He did. We are called to do even greater things than even Jesus, but the greatest miracle we may ever experience may just be letting the surgeon's hand go to work in our own lives and watching complete transformation come to pass.

I understand this helpless struggle, which lasted for thirty years of my life. I was waging an insidious battle. I didn't know that I was in bondage, but there was a time I had to make that same decision, and I had to do it by completely trusting the hand of God! It was an unknown place, a deep place in God.

I had just come out of a long relationship that left me feeling completely helpless and vulnerable. The relationship, which looked good from the outside, was so dysfunctional to the point of mental breakdown. I couldn't remember how to do things at my job that I could usually do with my eyes closed. I would black out and forget conversations I had just engaged in and even whole days. I had taken on so much with this relationship trying to please but enabling the victim. The outcome was I had become the victim.

It was the first time I had reached such a low point and critical mental condition, nearly having a mental breakdown, but it wasn't the first time I saw this pattern of behavior in my life. This pattern of behavior had traveled from relationship to relationship. I was running against time, wearing myself out, whittling down spiritually, and mentally trying to change. Instead, I was being conformed to the victims I had so desperately tried to rescue.

These things truly were meant for good. I always had good intentions. I was so deceived until I realized those patterns had always been there. I was born into this type of toxic thinking because my parents had never resolved their parents' toxic thinking. They gave me more than what they had, but I had been a carrier of generational oppression and disease!

God opened my eyes one winter.

I remember spending one Christmas with my family. It was all set up for us to enjoy a few weeks together. We rented a house, and I took a long vacation from work. We had many activities and adventures planned!

As with some family vacations, there are intense moments where attitudes or tempers fly, and there were a few moments like these in the beginning of the vacation. On the other hand, this was way out of the ordinary. In fact, with each day, those moments grew in number, and the intensity heightened. I was so frustrated! My mom would stay up sleepless nights, I would get lectured the next day, and my dad would brush it off, pretending it was nothing. I watched the way they communicated, and I couldn't help but truly see the dysfunction for the first time. What I thought was normal for every family was actually abnormal. This behavior was contrary to the way God created and intended the family unit to behave.

I remember having a sleepless night and praying to God, "God whatever is in them, I don't want in me. I need Your help."

I made the choice to completely surrender my life and had already made the decision to go through the internship through my church; I was so ready to break off these patterns of behavior. I didn't know what to do or how to do it, but I knew that the first step was surrender. So that night, I cried out to God, "I'm laying the cards on the table, God. I'm giving You everything, leaving nothing untouched by You. You get to have all of me."

God spoke to me a few weeks later as I was getting ready to join the internship. My pastor had already prophesied over me that God was going to heal me from the inside out. As I submitted to God, He spoke the most beautiful words:

"Dana, if you give Me your worst, I'll give you My best."

I didn't know what that action would bring, but the next year of my life was an incredible experience. The first day of internship, I went to lunch with my mentor and told her my whole story. God was so beautiful that He picked the most perfect woman to help me walk through this season of my life. I knew she was handpicked because I chose pastoral care on my own free will. As I stated previously, I had always leaned into the area of creative arts.

My mentor truly cared for me so well, but it didn't take a lot of prompting! That day, I told her point-blank that I knew I was dealing with generational oppression, I needed to get healed, I wanted her to give me the steps, and I would take them! She was so beautiful in the way she empowered me! It would have been detrimental to hold my hand and spoon-feed me! She knew the healing would come when I took the responsibility to go get my own healing, and I did!

I went to a few counseling sessions with a trusted Christian counselor to download everything to a third party. I remember being surprised at how compassionate the counselor was toward me and how she empathized with me. I saw so much of how I had been with other people now to reap my own reward. With the deepest compassion, she said, "Wow, Dana, you have really been through a lot. You should be so proud of yourself. You are really on the right trajectory. Good for you!"

I remember being so encouraged, so empowered, feeling so loved, and for the first time, recognizing everything I had been through. I had already overcome so much. I would be one of the first women in my family who had not contemplated or attempted suicide. I had always wanted to live despite the struggles! I didn't have that gene that everyone claims you have! I was the deal breaker! I was the one who would sever the cord of dysfunction in my family!

Maybe you have been waiting for days or years, but the waiting is over. Get up out of sickness, get up out of bondage, get up out of generational oppression, and walk in freedom!

Chapter 5

The Wound Has to Be Exposed

After the wound is addressed, it now has to be exposed. This stage involves the awakening process, which can be the most difficult and uncomfortable. We have no understanding of what to expect because we are coming up out of numbness for the first time.

Awakening from numbness is not an easy feat. It requires diligence and patience. We actually have to take the time to allow God to heal us by letting numbness go away and letting pain take its course. When we have numbed ourselves not to feel for a very long period of time, the minute we start to feel pain, we naturally want to retract and invert because that is how we are used to living. God graciously gives us a heightened awareness of this pain, but He is with us as we go through the process. He never leaves us or forsakes us in that process; in fact, He carries us.

Nothing illustrated this more than the vision God gave me for how we wake patients up in the ICU. This process parallels the process of waking up from numbness.

Each day in the ICU, we initiate a daily awakening trial. A daily awakening trial is essentially turning down the sedation on a patient until we start to see movement. The patient arouses to where we can assess their orientation and alertness to help us decide if they are neurologically intact and if they are fully awake. If their vitals are stable, we can actually wake them up and remove them from life support. They can breathe on their own and begin the recovery process.

This is much like when we wake up out of numbness. We anesthetize ourselves with coping mechanisms that have been in place to protect us from harm most of our lives, but these agents have actually kept us asleep. When we numb ourselves, we don't have to feel the pain of disappointment, hurt, low self-esteem, depression, guilt, fear, and shame. Essentially, we are like the walking dead, apathetic to change, apathetic to growth, and apathetic to how it affects us and those around us. We numb ourselves with busyness. We overcompensate by overworking or constantly pouring ourselves out, trying to fix others when it's actually us who need the fixing. Every hour of the day, every moment of space is accounted for so we don't have to process. We don't have to feel, we don't have to take responsibility, and we don't have to change. We can just be. Meanwhile, we are dying on the inside. We become dead to ourselves and, moreover, dead to others.

Waking up out of this numbness for the first time is a very unnatural feeling as it is for the ICU patient. Every ICU patient is different when they go through this process much like we are when waking up from numbness. Some wake up slowly but calm. They can be coached by those caring for them, "It's okay. You are just waking up. This is not an easy process. It is very uncomfortable, but if you participate, it won't be a long process. We can remove the life support, and you can breathe on your own. Unfortunately, we can't have you on any medications or sedation—you have to be fully awake to go through this process. We can't take you off life support if you are asleep—you won't be able to protect your airways and breathe on your own."

For some ICU patients, the awakening process is a real struggle. The moment they have an awareness that they are waking up, they immediately start thrashing, resisting, and trying to remove the foreign object (the endotracheal tube that helps them breathe). They cannot stand the fact that they have to deal with the foreign object that is present in their airway.

For some, it takes several people to coach them. They have to be restrained because they are so agitated and try to fight the nurses and medical staff. For some patients, you have to stand at their bedside through the whole process, coaching them, "It's okay. I know it's uncomfortable, but try to cooperate so this process does not have to take longer. We are here with you every step of the way. Don't fight the respirator or it will take longer until you can breathe on your own."

Like these ICU patients, the only way God can remove the foreign objects that are keeping us asleep is to take us through the awakening process. We want to go back to the default setting: the coping mechanisms, old mind-sets, and old ways of doing things to escape, but then we have to make the decision. Do we want to wake up? Are we willing to go through the process?

If we make the decision then and there, the struggle ceases, we become still, we lie in peace, we hear the still small voice of God, and we are completely aware of the pain. We can see the breakthrough on the other side. Eventually, the foreign objects that were causing the pain are removed, and we are finally set free from the anesthesia, the numbness, and we can breathe again, but this time on our own.

I clearly remember the night I was awakened. I was just a few weeks into my internship. I was at a creative team night on the altar. These creative team nights were designed for the entire creative arts team to come together in worship, have a supernatural encounter with God, and get a fresh word from heaven. There was ministry time at the end. I remember one of the worship leaders approached me and said, "Dana, you are here because God placed you here. It's not because of the worship pastor choosing you—God chose you. He has appointed you, but it is not by your might or by your power, but by His Spirit that you are here. You don't have to feel under qualified because He has qualified you."

It was right there in that moment that I truly felt I understood grace for the first time because I actually received it. I had many words spoken over me during the course of my life, but I never fully believed them because of all the guilt, condemnation, and shame. On the other hand, this word was different. Something on the inside of me literally awakened. For the first time, I truly believed I was both chosen and qualified. Receiving that grace meant that I didn't have to assume the responsibility of qualifying myself because Christ had already assumed it. I simply had to believe.

As euphoric as that experience was, I had no idea what would happen next. Just like the patient waking up in the ICU and becoming aware of the foreign object in their airway, I became aware of the foreign things that had been oppressing me for nearly thirty years.

That night, as I was in my bathroom, meditating on the experience at the altar, I heard the Holy Spirit say, "Now you are ready."

At that moment, He began to flood my mind with every traumatic memory that occurred in my childhood, and I felt a level of pain I had never experienced. The only way I can describe the traumatic events that saturated my mind were they were like someone flipping through a comic book of all the scenes of my life I had forgotten, scenes I had repressed. I spun out of control, my mind was racing, and my heart was beating so fast! I was weeping uncontrollably in a fetal position on the floor, unable to even describe all the emotions I was feeling at once, the full expression of repressed pain.

I remembered shouting out, "But, God, I forgave!" And the Holy Spirit replied, "You did forgive, but we didn't deal with what happened to you."

Notice that He said, "We didn't deal." It was the most intense pain I had ever felt, but I knew I was not alone in this process. The Holy Spirit would be with me every step of the way. What I understood at that time was that he had to wait until I was spiritually mature enough to handle what He had to show me. If it had been any time before actually receiving His grace, I would have been in complete denial. The Lord knew what He was doing; He set me up to heal me.

To stay awake, there are some things that we have to understand. These are things that most people are not taught, and they quickly fall back into numbness.

During the early stages of awakening patients in the ICU, the nurses have to stay with them, monitor them very closely, make sure they can secure their airway, and breathe on their own. Sometimes, the sedation is still clearing, so we have to ensure the patient does not fall back asleep.

People need to be closely monitored and watched when they wake up from numbness. They need to have a great connection with people in their faith communities or they too will fall back asleep. There is still a struggle to stay awake, to stay healed, but having these networks in place will keep that person from falling back asleep.

Chapter 6

Tears Lubricate the Wound

The healing process is something that we should look forward to, but for most people, they are fearful of what comes next. They have no idea the battle they are about to engage in or the outcome. Will they get free? Will they be healed? How long does this take? The vulnerability is frightening; they are hopeful but scared out of their mind. They are willing, but their flesh is weak. They want freedom's reward, but that freedom comes with a cost! On the other hand, the payoff will last forever if they are willing to stay the journey.

What if I were to tell you that restoration and healing are a mountaintop experience? What if I were to tell you that when we go through the deepest pain, we experience the greatest joy and the deepest intimacy with God? It is indeed the safest we will ever feel. Although we are being healed from the inside out and we are going through what seems like emotional turmoil, this is actually the resting phase of healing. It is truly in this deeply dependent place that our soul finds its good shepherd who leads us besides still waters and provides rest for our soul. The resting phase begins in the place of complete dependence. If we are looking at the big picture, we can't enjoy this part of the journey. This part of the journey is not meant to be endured, but enjoyed.

Hebrews 12:2 (NKJV) says, "Jesus, the author and finisher of our faith, who for the joy that was set before Him endured the cross, despising the shame, and has sat down at the right hand of the throne of God."

Jesus had to go through the process of crucifixion so he could experience the resurrection; this is much like the process of healing. The weight of unaddressed pain and its consequences have plagued us for so long! We have to go through the process of crucifying that pain so we can experience total healing. Jesus went through the process full of joy, and so can we.

James 1:2–4 (NKJV) says, "My brethren, count it all joy when you fall into various trials, knowing that the testing of your faith produces patience. But let patience have its perfect work, that you may be perfect and complete, lacking nothing."

James 1:2–4 (MSG) translation goes further to say, "Under pressure, your faith-life is forced into the open and shows its true colors. Don't try to get out of anything prematurely, let it do its work so you become mature and well developed, not deficient in any way."

Psalms 91:1 (NKJV) says, "He who dwells in the secret place of the Most High Shall abide under the shadow of the Almighty."

As previously described, the day I was in a patient's room caring for a deeply infected wound, the Holy Spirit revealed the next step of the wound healing process. As nurses at the bedside in the natural, the first step is identifying the wound and what is causing it. Then we proceed to uncovering the wound and exposing it. Now the next step is cleansing the wound.

When we begin this process as nurses, we have taken all the bandages off, and the wound is exposed. Now we need to irrigate the wound with normal saline. Normal saline is used as an irrigant to begin to slough off all of the necrosed dead tissue so that we eventually get down to the viable tissue; this is how a wound heals from the inside out.

While this is a process I understand from the natural perspective of being a bedside nurse, the Holy Spirit showed me that this coincides with healing in the spiritual. Just as we use salt water in the natural to irrigate the wound, removing excess dead tissue, hardness, slough, infection, and any contaminants, we also do the same in the spiritual sense. We use saline rinses in the natural, but in the spiritual, we use our tears to accomplish the removal of the rough calloused areas of our hearts. Our tears are salt water!

I am dedicating an entire chapter to the process of grieving because we need to understand that grieving is a very important part of the healing process. In fact, you can't heal without tears, just like wounds can't heal in the natural without being irrigated by normal saline!

Can we be released? We need to understand that is okay to cry, and it is not weakness! We have all heard the saying that laughter is the best medicine, but let me tell you tears are a close follower. In fact, it is very hard to grieve in this process without experiencing joy on the other side!

The Bible speaks over and over again about tears and joy; those two things come in a pair! Psalms 30:5 (NKJV) says, "Weeping may endure for a night, but joy comes in the morning."

Psalm 126:5 (NKJV) says, "Those who sow in tears shall reap in joy. He who continuously goes forth weeping, bearing seed for sowing, shall doubtless come again with rejoicing."

Here's a really powerful one: John 11:35 (NKJV) says, "Jesus wept!" Jesus himself wept! Jesus experienced pain! Jesus grieved and Jesus overcame!

There is truly only one way to lubricate and cleanse a wound. We have to grieve! We have to express our emotions, or we will repress them.

This part of the process is so essential for complete healing, but it is the part that seems to be the most difficult for anyone I have ministered to, whether in the hospital, in the community, or in the church body. The minute they begin to cry, they pull back in restraint and they shut down until I give them permission to cry.

Why does this happen? This happens because for most of us, this was the coping mechanism we put in place as children to protect ourselves from rejection, abuse, and hurt. Perhaps, like me, we had to be the savior of our victimized families so someone had to hold it together; someone had to be strong.

We think this is a sign of strength, but it becomes our greatest enemy in adulthood when the repressed pain, unexpressed, begins to manifest itself in our behaviors. Our outward appearance begins to demonstrate what is happening on the inside.

I remember going through a very painful process in my early twenties. I had rebelled out of unaddressed hurt and pain, and had to face the consequences of my poor behavior. I had worked tirelessly for so long to hold my family together and to try to hold myself together but began to lose the battle at a very rapid rate. I remember being on the phone with my dad, trying to explain everything that was happening to me. I became so overwhelmed with fear and the chaos that was happening in my life that I couldn't calm myself down. All of a sudden, it was like the floodgates opened; I could no longer hold it inside. I began to sob uncontrollably in an almost panicked state. My dad didn't know what to do, so he handed the phone to my mom, who couldn't calm me down either. It was such an overwhelming state; I literally felt like I was going to have a nervous breakdown. I remember shouting, gasping for breath in between saying, "I just need to cry! I just need to cry!"

This is an excellent demonstration of what happens when we don't deal with our emotions properly. We lose control because we are trying so hard to keep control. What has really happened is that fear begins to control us, and we begin acting out of the root of fear!

So let's fast-forward to what grieving should look like when we let pain take its natural course. To begin to understand the grieving process, we have to know from the beginning that there are physical manifestations that we must go through! Most people are completely left in the dark and think that something is terribly wrong when they start to get the emotional instability, the nausea, and the headaches. This is what is expected! Everyone does grieve differently, but remember we were numb for a very long time! We have never allowed ourselves to express emotions properly. Now we are allowing God to wash us and to cleanse away all the calloused areas of our hearts so we can live unrestricted. If we are experiencing some discomfort, we must remember that healing and grieving are never comfortable, but God is releasing us to let go and let Him take care of us! Remember, it is not the well that needs a physician but the sick. We need to let the great physician help us get healthy again. Remember, it's supposed to be messy.

It was certainly a messy process for me, but I want you to know how real this stuff is so that you feel empowered to allow yourself to heal as the Holy Spirit tenderly leads!

Every Tuesday, we would have a staff meeting with all of the church staff, interns, and volunteers. The atmosphere at these staff meetings was often so thick with the presence of God and had a completely different feel than weekend meetings. Often, our pastor had prophetic words, and the environment was conducive to healing and breakthrough. The worship was so intense and intimate!

During the meetings, I would often find myself getting stirred up; it was the feeling of being washed. I knew that God was dealing with the demonic because I would often get headaches or nausea, or just begin to cry. I would have to quietly get up from my seat and go to the restroom, where I would dry heave. Sometimes, I would just have to wash my face and do some deep breathing. Other times, I would just have to let the tears flow because it was uncontrollable; I had never experienced this emotion. The tears would sometimes start and I couldn't stop. In the beginning, it was so tough to try to control my emotions, but at that point, it wasn't necessary.

Once I got a handle on the nausea and the tears, I discreetly let myself back into the meeting. I did this for a good six months, but I kept coming back, while God helped me not to let my emotions run the day. I dealt with them as they came but really hadn't been prepared for that part of it.

Conveniently, I had quite a commute at times to worship practices, connect groups, or church services. God literally used this as a vehicle to let it all go. I would cry until I felt like I had completely emptied out. Most of the time, I had no clue why I was even crying, but I felt that most of it was letting go. Because I had been so shut up for so long, when the time came, the tears were like a river. They just kept flowing and flowing! I didn't know when they were going to end, but for the first time, I didn't stop them. The release was so freeing! I understood the peace that surpasses understanding. I would feel unspeakable joy because I was in complete surrender. I was completely undone. God took special care of me; he unraveled me from the inside out.

In the beginning, I would cry upon waking, cry at various points throughout the day, cry when I commuted in my car both ways, and cry myself to sleep. The only way to describe this was my heart, prior to this, was like a car frozen over in the winter. When I began to cry, it was like someone turned on the defrost button. The more I cried, the longer I stuck to the grieving process! I let pain take its course, and my vision started to become clear, just like a car does when it has been completely defrosted.

I would even ask my mentor, "Is this normal? I can't stop crying!" She gently replied, "Dana, you have been shut up your whole life, holding on to as much as you can hold on to. Just let go, let the tears flow like a river, and don't try to understand or control it."

Later, we would laugh, as I would joke about not having my daily cry. If I didn't cry for a week, I was surely overdue for a meltdown.

This is the beautiful thing about the grace God gives us during this process. Later, I was asked by so many people how I went through what I did because they saw no evidence. I told them that God was so faithful to give me the grace, time, and space I needed to grieve.

God does this uniquely for every person in such a way that when we come out on the other side, we really can't explain how we did it, but we feel the best we have ever felt in our lives! For me, grieving went from several times a day in just the right places, to once a day, to a few times a week, to once a week, to once a month. Somehow, I always had a means of excusing myself or a place to go get alone with God, meditate, pray, and grieve. It was so beautiful! It truly was a mountaintop experience, a type of euphoria that cannot be explained until it is experienced. I was nestled in the arms of Jesus; He carried me. I was exposed openly and publicly, but won battles privately.

Some people have asked me if they would be able to work. They were afraid that by feeling for the first time and awakening from numbness, they might not be able to function or be too overwhelmed. The truth is there were times where I literally felt like I couldn't function, but I had to depend on the supernatural strength of the Holy Spirit to accomplish what I could not accomplish. Not only did I work full time but also I interned in pastoral care full time and I served on the worship team, which is one of the most time-consuming ministries in church! Somehow, I had all the space I needed to grieve with just a few exceptions of having to walk out of rehearsal to get my bearings or miss a few meetings. Over the course of a year, God unraveled me, and He healed me from the inside out.

Chapter 7

It Gets Messy before It Gets Better

    The counselor began to walk me through the steps of loving my family from a distance and learning to set healthy boundaries. I knew that I was going to have to spend some time away to allow myself to heal properly, I had to disconnect myself from the source of affliction, and I had to go from low-functioning toxic relationships to high-functioning healthy relationships. It didn't make much sense at the time. I would ask God why I needed to be separated from my earthly family. After all, He put us together here on this earth. It was then I realized all the guilt, shame, and condemnation I had been carrying around for nearly thirty years. The only way to expose the wound and take off the hard coverings was to get alone with God. I was fearful because I had always been the savior of my family. What would they do without me there at the beckoning of their call? Who would stand up for what was right? Who would pray and believe? They seemed so helpless, but was it them, or was it me?

    Earlier in the year, I had booked a flight home for a vacation in the Outer Banks where I grew up. Almost immediately, even as my fingers were clicking the confirmation of the flight, I began to regret my decision. I began to have inward remorse; the same nausea and headaches returned. I truly didn't feel that this was a wise decision. I ignored that feeling and proceeded with my plans to go home. After all, it was a family vacation. I could handle it for a week; I was strong. But then God began to deal with me, and He did it through other people. Every time I would begin telling people about the trip home, I would begin to cry and transparently say, "I really don't want to go, but I feel like I have no choice." Close friends would say, "Dana, do you have to go? You don't have to go." Inside, I was agreeing, but I didn't feel like I had the guts to do it. I had never said no to my family! During that time, and even since the beginning of the healing process, my mother would send very toxic, lengthy text messages communicating that I should feel guilty, reminding me of what I wasn't doing or who I wasn't. She would post stuff on social media; the language grew more and more toxic. Normally, there would be phases of this, but I would simply assume it was only a short-term phase. She would get over it; we would talk about it, apologize, forgive, and be done with it until the next time. I had been so used to this that initially I applied my previous experience to this situation. But now that the wound was exposed, as the Holy Spirit started leading and giving me wisdom, I knew now my response needed to change. I started ignoring the text messages and the voicemails. I wouldn't open them when they came in. At first, it was quite a discipline, but as God strengthened me, I grew stronger.

After several messages came through, I would simply reply, "Mom, I'm not reading these. I don't have to receive these words and I can't afford to have these things spoken over my life. I'm sorry."

Needless to say, this was not received very well, and those text messages and voicemails began to get more verbally abusive. At that time, I was still seeing the counselor, so when I explained these to her, she looked at me and said, "Dana, you do not have to go home." My heart was starting to make the shift, but I wasn't quite ready to make the decision.

Then just a few nights later, my decision was changed through a prophetic dream. In the dream, I was running frantically from something I couldn't see. My clothes were torn to shreds, and I had been beaten nearly to death. I ran into the house of my mentor and searched for her everywhere, but I couldn't find her anywhere. I was screaming that someone or something was trying to kill me. After searching and not finding her, I ran out of the house and straight into Tiananmen Square in China. I recognized it because I had traveled there a few years prior but didn't know why it was in this dream. What I did see were my senior pastors standing in the middle of the square. I ran to them frantically just like I had in my mentor's house. I was talking a thousand miles a minute in a state of panic, saying, "Help me! Someone is trying to kill me! Look at me! I have been beaten nearly to death." The entire time I was talking, my senior pastor was trying to calm me down. Finally, he got firm with me and said, "Dana, stop! Stop! Calm down! This is a spirit!"

Immediately, my eyes opened, and I realized that Tiananmen Square actually represented the demonic realm. There is a tremendous amount of demonic activity in these areas of the world, but my senior pastors, my shepherds, were standing in the middle of that realm and protecting me. I knew then that what I had felt in my spirit, what my close friends had confirmed, what my counselor had confirmed, and now this very prophetic dream had confirmed, was that I did not need to step back into the pit that from which I had been rescued. The next thing I would do was one of the hardest decisions I have ever had to make but would change the trajectory of my life.

I knew I had to communicate this to my family and I had to do it quickly. I couldn't shrink back; I couldn't back down. I had to act. I remember I was working that day. It was not my normal to text anyone anything of great importance requiring a face-to-face or at least a telephone conversation, but I knew it would not go over well. The only way to truly get it all out on the table was to text my mom. I texted her a very simple message. I basically told her that I did not have a good feeling about coming home and, after much thought, I would have to cancel my trip. I hoped that she would understand.

I felt faith and fear all at the same time. I felt sorrow and joy. Mostly, I felt strengthened. I had finally said no; I had finally colored outside of the lines. This was the beginning of the boundary setting my counselor spoke with me about.

Just as I thought, it did not go well. I couldn't even read more than just a few of the lines my mother texted me. They were words I felt the enemy was speaking to me; they were sickening. Despite that sickening feeling, I felt lighter because the decision had been made. I didn't know what to expect next, but I knew this one was big!

That night, I took communion and laid everything at the feet of Jesus and said, "God, I do not receive any of these words spoken to me, and I break the spirit behind them in Jesus's name." Those words were disempowered; they no longer had any stronghold over my life. My life was blessed, not cursed.

This was when I stepped into the next phase of healing. After the dream, I now knew what I was dealing with. It was not the words or actions of my mom but the demonic spirit living on the inside of her at that time.

The demonic spirit was controlling her; it reigned over her life. It governed her mind, thoughts, and words, and the fields of her heart. The demonic spirit spoke through her. I was no longer dealing with my mom; I was taking authority over the demonic spirit, breaking its power!

At my last counseling session, we talked about the next steps and how to begin loving my family from a distance. She suggested that every month, I send my mom a card, words of affirmation, or do something nice for her. I began to speak words of affirmation over my mom, speaking to her potential, and not her behavior. Eventually, I did send her cards with encouraging words.

The hardest part was facing the disappointment of my father as he was losing his brother to cancer. He lacked understanding of why his little girl, his greatest gift, would leave at such a time. Why would she not come home? What had he done? He was already in such a melancholic state. I had to not think about the sadness in his voice when he said, "Dana, I guess you have to do what you have to do, but I don't understand."

This wasn't the best timing, but I still couldn't shrink back when it came to these circumstances because it was God's time to heal my family and me. I had to tell my father, "Dad, I know you don't understand. I know you are facing the worst of circumstances, but you have to know that I am in complete obedience to God. I am doing this because I love you, and something has to change." My dad began to cry and he couldn't talk on the phone. This was one of the toughest conversations I have ever had with my dad, but if I wanted to heal, I had to get real, be strong, and be courageous.

About a week after, I had made the decision not to go home; I was still very heavy with the weight of that decision. We held our women's ministry meetings monthly, and this particular one was very timely. My mentor spoke a very prophetic message titled "Just Give Them Jesus." She spoke about people carrying burdens they were never meant to carry. She talked about how she discipled and counseled several women who were dealing with familiar demonic spirits, which particularly affected relationships between a mother and a daughter. This was definitely a serious issue in this generation of women, both young and old, that needed attention. In her message, she walked us through the steps that we would need not to take on the unnecessary burdens of generational oppression but to point our families to Jesus, the one true answer to everything we could ever face. At the end, she gave an altar call for women who had been carrying and suffering from these burdens. I was normally on the ministry team, but now this was my time. I had made the decision and I had executed it. Now it was time to completely lay it on the altar.

I don't think I even ran to the altar! I believe I crawled there! I remember being on my face, weeping, my chest heaving, letting it all go once and for all. It wasn't pretty. In fact, it was pretty messy. One of the beautiful women's ministry leaders who knew my situation knelt down beside me and held me in her arms as I continued to sob and moan. I remember I had a fistful of snot! I didn't care who was there and I didn't care what I looked like! I just wanted to leave it all on the altar once and for all!

This woman's gentle, soothing words and her human touch were straight from the mouth and hands of God. She was the voice of an angel, and she spoke to me gently, but full of faith. It was so refreshing to feel her arms come around me in my lowest of times, knowing she had celebrated me in the highest as well.

God was so faithful to bring loving people around me during that time. That day, I stood up, wiped the tears, wiped away the snot, and began to hold my head high. I had a confidence I hadn't had, a hope, and an assurance. Circumstances would shift; I could see the mountaintop.

I wish I could say the texts and e-mails stopped, but, honestly, they grew worse and were more venomous than ever. I had to block my mom from social media. It hurt me so much to do so, but I couldn't afford it for myself or to expose other people in my influence and leadership.

Threats would often come from my mom. This was where I came to the place of deep trust in God. My mom would say things like "You have ruined my life. I'm going to end it, and it's going to be all your fault," or she said, "I can't believe you deserted and left your family for your new family" (as she was referring to my church family).

The fearful thoughts would come: *God, what if she takes her life?* But then I would pray a prayer of protection over her and myself. I would hear the still small voice of God say, "Dana, you are going to have to let go and trust Me with your family." He would frequently remind me of that when the hopeless thoughts would come, and again, I would be filled with hope and peace. I knew that my mom's life would be spared and that God would cover and protect her. The more I exercised my language of faith in this area, the more my trust developed. This was life and death, but God had met me in this place, and I knew He wouldn't fail me. I could trust Him to heal me and heal my family.

Then one night, God gave me a word that I would stand on during this season. As I lay in my bed getting ready to go to sleep, I flipped open my Bible, and the pages randomly landed in Isaiah 30:19 (NKJV) and said, "You shall weep no more. He will be very gracious to you at the sound of your cry; When he hears it, he will answer you. And though the Lord gives you the bread of adversity and the water of affliction, Yet your teachers will not be moved into a corner anymore, But your eyes shall see your teachers. Your ears shall hear a word behind you, saying, 'This is the way, walk in it.'"

God was saying He had indeed heard my cry and He had answered it with His Word, His promise: to listen to His still small voice and instruction, then obey. Further down in Isaiah 30:23 (NKJV), He went on to say, "Then He will give you the rain for your seed With which you sow the ground, and bread of the increase of the earth; It will be fat and plentiful." Skipping down to verse 25, "There will be on every high mountain And on every high hill Rivers and streams of waters, In the day of the great slaughter, When the towers fall. Moreover the light of the moon will be as the light of the sun, And the light of the moon will be sevenfold As the light of seven days, In the day that the Lord binds of the bruise of His people And heals the stroke of their wound."

In other words, God was saying to me, "Girlfriend, stay on the course, listen to Me, and let Me guide you. Keep sowing, the rain is coming. See the mountaintop. See your greatest nightmare turn into your wildest dream because this is what I see. Go through this process, see Me provide, see Me bless, see the fruit of the season spring forth, and remain. But hold on, I need to heal you first."

Binding up the bruise of his people and the stroke of their wound meant God would fully heal and restore my family and me. I had his word. People are like the grass that withers and the flowers that fade, but the Word of God is eternal and it remains. This would be the word that I would recite over and over, the word that kept me grounded, the word that was unshakable on the inside of me. This is where trust was found and kept.

I was beginning to come alive again. The one thing that returned to me was sleep. There had been years of sleepless nights, tormenting dreams, worry, anxiety, fear, and racing thoughts that occurred almost constantly. For the first time in years, my mind properly shut down at night. I would fall asleep and not wake up until seven or eight hours later. This rest was necessary for the emotional battles I had to fight; it gave me physical strength and endurance. This rest was also a sign of God's peace. Because I had given Him lordship in my life to deal with the things that needed to be dealt with, I could experience His peace as He intended. I would even tell my mentor, "Wow! I can't believe how easily the sleep comes and the incredible dreams He brings to me each night!" She said, "Now that God has begun to heal you and take away the guilt, shame, and condemnation, He can fill your mind with His thoughts, with His dreams, and with His words for you."

That couldn't be truer. Not only was He giving me more dreams, visions, and His reality but also He was putting so much of His Word inside of me. I would speak with authority, I would pray with authority, and I would meditate on His word night and day. His Word became a very natural part of my language. His Word had begun to clean up the clutter and congestion of my mind and heart. His Word now had access to live inside of me and had the ability to easily permeate my mind and heart. I began to gain a true understanding of His heart and His thoughts, not just for myself but for the people He had placed into my care. I began to have a real understanding of not just His works but also His ways. I began to understand the character of God and could see it expressed through me.

Things started to truly shift, and I found myself not so inwardly focused. It started to project on the outside. I am not the type of person who can really hide what I am thinking. My mentor would always laugh and say, "Dana, I never have to worry about where you are—it always shows on your face." She could easily discern where I was spiritually and would address it as needed, but often I could self-correct with the help of the Holy Spirit. It was often me going to her instead of her coming to me; that's a true sign of the work of the Holy Spirit!

I felt the most loved by God in his correction. He never spoke condemnation but as a Father who truly loved and wanted the best for His daughter. The correction was easily received and easily shifted. I was completely immersed, all in, absorbing everything my Father wanted to tell me and show me so that I could show others His unfailing love.

Things do grow worse before they get better. Sometimes, on the uprise, there is a bump in the road. On the other hand, once we get our footing with the Word of God, the roots of his words go deep inside of us so circumstances can't come knock us over. I was like an oak tree, firmly planted.

About nine months into this intense healing process, I still had very little contact with my family. While it seemed to get better over time, as I gained strength and wisdom, November came, which would be their birthday month. When their birthdays came, it felt like more of a funeral. This walking away felt like I had actually lost them, like they had passed away. I remember telling God that if the price for healing and freedom required me to continue to do this for a great length of time, I would pay it because I had His Word; He would heal my family and me so I would see them again. But just like when you lose a loved one, when their birthdays come around, we mourn and grieve for them, and this is what happened to me one weekend in November.

I felt the impending doom driving home from work on a Friday night. The flights of tears were now coming less often and less frequently, but I felt a significant surge of tears rise on the inside of me on the way home. My heart ached and my soul grieved. I started to think about them. For the first time, a healthy condition manifested itself; I actually missed them. I began to sob; my heart's cry for them was so loud. I wanted so badly to see them, to talk to them, to have a somewhat normal moment with them, but realized the process was still in place. I still had to be obedient and listen to the wisdom of that still small voice.

I lay on my couch most of the next day, crying, sleeping, waking up, crying again, and then dreading to go to church that night. I felt like I could barely lift my head. I felt like I barely had any strength. I felt the sorrow. I felt the depression, but I knew that I had to get to church, even if I had to crawl inside of the doors. I had to get there and I had to worship.

I had been here before, wiping away the tears. It wasn't a facade; I had to overcome the emotions, and that's what I did! I got up. I showered, washed my face, put on something amazing, and made the thirty-minute drive to be in an atmosphere of breakthrough and to get a word from God. And I did it with a big smile on my face!

I will never forget that night at church. In worship, the Holy Spirit ministered to me. He was healing the broken places, He was fixing the misaligned things, and He was restoring my soul. If worship wasn't already an incredible experience, the biggest surprise came next. After a time of prayer, we all went back to our seats after a one-minute meet and greet. It was then that my beautiful senior pastor, who once stood for me in the middle of the demonic realm, approached me with a small Tiffany's bag and said, "Dana, I was praying and really felt God wanted me to give you this gift! It's just a small token of our appreciation for you. Thank you so much for shepherding and taking such great care of people." I was completely blown away. I knew my senior pastor was pretty prophetic, but God had sent her to bless me during one of the hardest weekends of my healing process. She didn't know about the tears, the mourning, the grieving, and the weighted decision to clean up and turn up, but God's love was expressed for me so deeply through her obedience. This gift was a sign and a token of God's provision in this season. I would put her card in my "blessings" drawer and, on occasion, open it and remind myself of God's provision for me during my time of need.

The following week, I decided it was now time for someone in my family to make a move forward, and I would make the first communication. It was Veteran's Day. My dad was a veteran, so I used this as an excuse to call home. I simply wanted to thank him for his service for our country and for risking his life.

I was at work at the time, so I thought I would make a quick call home. It would be short and sweet and would get the ball rolling. Nervously, I dialed the number, and after two rings, my mother answered the phone. Her voice was distant and weak; she seemed a bit confused. She thought I was a telemarketer because I called from work. When she heard my voice again, she said, "Dana, is that you?" I paused for a few seconds because I hadn't expected her to pick up the phone, but I replied, "Yes, it's me."

She paused for a few minutes and she said, "Well, how are you?"

I felt the tears begin to come. Choking them back, I replied, "I'm okay. I didn't expect you to answer the phone. I was calling to wish Dad a Happy Veteran's Day."

She mentioned something about him being outside working, and then the conversation began to progress. The tears began to come, and I said, "Mom, the last few months have been some of the hardest months of my life. I really have felt like I had lost you. It's like you had passed away. When your birthdays came, I was a mess—I mourned for you."

My mom began crying to the point of not being able to form words, but when she did, the words she said would be the answer to years and months of prayer. It was well worth all of the labor in tears.

She said, "Dana, it's been hard for us too, but I now know that you did the right thing. What you did was right and you did it because you loved us. I now know how much you love us and I am so sorry for everything I said to you. You needed to do that, but what you didn't know is that while this was all going on, God sent people. I started seeing the family practitioner (a Christian physician) when all of this was going on. I told him everything that had been going on, and he reached out and said, 'This is not normal, and this is not okay. Why don't you let me help you?'"

You see, God's promises were true! I could trust Him with my family; it was me that had to be removed from the situation so that He could get to them. In my desperation to save them, I was in the way of the miracle. So while God set me aside to heal me, He did as He promised, and He sent people. Not only did our family physician step out to try to get to the root of the situation but also my mom was able to start seeing a Christian psychiatrist who would pray for her, not wanting to further medicate her but to get rid of the root once and for all!

At this time, my parents also started to attend Freedom House Church in Virginia, a church that God had put on my cousin's heart to plant. The amazing thing about it was that God had given me a word of knowledge at a conference that my family would be part of a church plant; it would come through my cousin. This had now come to pass, and this church was everything I had prayed for my family to find. This church was a spirit-filled, life-giving church, much like the one I was attending. My parents were able to finally plant themselves in good, healthy soil. They were now free from the guilt, shame, and condemning fear-based churches they had attended prior. They would now know how to operate from the victory they already had in Christ and break the bondages they had been living with once and for all!

That conversation was like a breath of fresh air as I was able to talk to my dad. I found out how much God had been working and moving behind the scenes! Although I knew the battle was not nearly over, I was reassured that I did discern what God was telling me to do, and the obedience was paying off.

Even though I could see God moving, I still had to use wisdom in communication and boundary setting with my family. Even though the toxic texts and e-mails had stopped, I was not quick to open the doors yet. I would contact them every few weeks, and my mom would send much shorter texts here and there, but they were not toxic or abusive.

About a month or so later, we received news that my uncle who had been in remission from cancer was sick again. When he was admitted to the hospital, the scans came back showing cancer all over his body and into his bones. They said his prognosis was very poor and he had days to weeks.

The family all came together in the hospital, and they put him on comfort care, allowing each family member the opportunity to spend time with him and say goodbye. I fasted and prayed for my family. I encouraged them to press in for a miracle, but after a little over a week, I received a call at work that my uncle had passed away. I tried to talk to my father, but he couldn't even make words out. He was in a fetal position on the floor having lost his closest brother and one of his best friends.

I now knew that it was time to make the trip home. I had to take everything that I had learned and apply it. I needed to go home to be with my dad and comfort him during this time, but I knew I was not on my turf. I would have to set boundaries if needed. I got some of the people on my pastoral team to pray with me, including my mentor, as it would be hard to go back into this environment again. I felt very ready to face it and handle it.

My brother picked me up at the airport, and we drove straight to the family viewing for my uncle. When we arrived, I found my dad, went straight to him, and hugged him. He looked very haggard and very far from his normal. I looked around and was completely disturbed at the appearances of my family members. Many appeared far beyond their ages from years of hard living. Many seemed broken, apathetic, and disengaged.

Even from the beginning, I had to put boundaries in place as my mom was trying to control the situation. I had to respectfully remind her that this wasn't about her. I spent the first night with my brother and went with him to the funeral the next day. This funeral wasn't just any funeral. My cousin and uncles brought several words of encouragement and a call to salvation. A salvation invitation was given to our entire family, and there was an incredible response. God truly does work all things for good even in death. We spent the day with family at a gathering after the service, and then I rode home with my dad. I tried not to talk too much about anything because I didn't want to cause any more discomfort.

When we got home, my mom was, at first, very silent and distant. She was not happy at all with me cutting her off the night before and standing my ground. The silence was soon broken, and she laid into me about my confrontation with her. Again, I was firm, setting boundaries, while asking the Holy Spirit for wisdom on every answer. I made sure my responses were well thought out. That went on almost the entire time. I constantly had to pray. I went to bed most nights crying but still had the peace of God in the situation.

I spent the next night with one of my best friends. On return, I came home and found my mom sitting in her chair. She was in an inebriated state, very drowsy, and her words were slurred. She asked me a few questions about my visit, and then her eyes narrowed. She began to lay into me about my abandonment of them over the last few months. Again, it was that same demonic spirit speaking through her, but this time it could not reach me or penetrate me. I confronted it, standing my ground and speaking boldly with the authority of who I was in Christ. Then I went to bed.

The next morning, my mother did not even recall me coming in the night before. I felt, in that moment, it wasn't the time to confront in truth. Overall, that day was one of the best days that we had. God continued to be with me. I got to spend some time with my dad and could now talk to him about what I saw. He had been using coping mechanisms to numb the pain for years, and I demonstrated that to him by touching him in different places on his arm. I said, "Dad, physically, you can feel me prick your arms, but spiritually, you can't feel this." I told him that unknowingly, he has tried to maintain for years with the same coping mechanisms. Now they were no longer effective and they had begun to affect him physically. I let him know that it was okay to grieve the death of his brother and everything he had gone through in the past decade. I encouraged him to allow God to take the numbness away and go through the course of pain. I didn't want to see what started off as trying to cope or take the edge off turn into a disease with a long road to recovery. I let him know that it was now his time to heal, that he could let go, that crying was okay and it wasn't weakness, and that he had a hope and a future.

On the morning of my departure flight, I had breakfast with my family. I began speaking into their lives, prophesying over them, and letting them know that I had been awake early every morning praying over their household, releasing healing, restoration, and peace.

I prayed over each of them with a word from God, and then it was time to tell my mom about the conversation from two nights before. The whole time I had been home, her confession had been that her mind was being healed, she no longer dealt with demonic thoughts, and she was in a good place. While I did want to encourage her to speak life over herself, I did not want to keep her in the dark. I let her know about the state I had found her in, some of the things that she had said, and my response to her. I truthfully, in love, told her that there were still some very serious issues that I would not leave without addressing. Now knowing what I was dealing with, it actually allowed me to love her more by loving her through it. On the other hand, she would only be able to move forward once she made the decision for herself. I knew this was Jesus because it was so well received. She thanked me for confronting something that was probably very uncomfortable. She was apologetic and really wanted to work on it. I reminded her of what I had to do, and she was optimistic to apply the wisdom.

That was a turning point for my family! I had now gone, stood in the middle of the stronghold, grounded in the promises and Word of God, and directed by the wisdom of the Holy Spirit. I truly felt God was fighting for me in that place, and nothing could by any means harm me. Nothing was against me. I was upheld by his righteousness!

My mom and dad began to send me great reports of God breaking things off at church and in counseling sessions. My dad was still pretty heavily burdened and grieved from my uncle's death, but he was going through the healing process. He was so appreciative of me coming home to spend that time with him. My mom said, overall, he was really in a better place. My mom continued to confront things in her life and was beginning to experience freedom. They both got very planted and started serving at Freedom House church. Other family members were now coming to my cousin's church; the course had really started to shift onward and upward. I was able to contact and communicate with my family more and more. They were very open to wisdom and counsel as I gently gave it. I only went as far as they were ready to receive. God was beginning to fill my mom's mind with his thoughts and his plans for her just as he did for me.

I truly saw the fruit of it all when we stepped out for a family vacation. I invited my parents to stay with me and come to our third annual Empower conference. Honestly, it was a step of faith because I was very nervous and fearful, but I had to release it and let God be God. We had to give it a go, and I truly did not want to put them in a hotel; I had a place where they could stay in one of the best parts of town.

The vacation was incredible! The parents that I picked up from the airport were two different people! I was late to the airport because I had been getting stuff ready for the conference, but they were totally fine with it! We got them settled in and had a great walk, chat, and dinner. We stayed up just talking and laughing. My cousin and his wife would be in town as well, attending the conference as VIP pastors.

I served a lot over the next few days, but my parents were content doing their own thing and meeting up with my cousins. I would meet up with them in the evenings, and we would go out for boardwalk strolls and dinners. Let me tell you, they were normal family dinners!

After the conference, they were all invited up to the VIP pastors' green room lounge since it was the last night. They were able to meet my pastors and church family. We hung out and relaxed before taking my cousins to the airport.

I will never forget a moment that we had in the green room that night. I was reminded of how much God loved me by how He demonstrated it through my senior pastor, an incredible shepherd and a faithful, humble servant. My church family had already treated my family like their own, but this particular moment with my senior pastor was so touching.

As my cousin was saying his goodbyes, my pastor looked up from where he was. He was with his dearest friends, celebrating an incredible conference and move of God. When he saw my family start to say their goodbyes, he got up from where he was, came, and talked to my cousins. They exchanged contact information, and then he met my father.

He went on to say the sweetest, most precious things about me. Nothing was more moving than watching the encounter with my spiritual father and my earthly father. My senior pastor reassured my father that he would make sure I was well looked after, that they would make sure I found the right guy and the right house (as I had been in the market to buy my first home).

I could see that this was hard for my dad, as he was unable to be there physically for this, but what an incredible exchange this was, and a divine appointment. I had never felt more loved than when I observed how my church family and pastors took such great care of my family. I was so loved and so blessed. I understood why my pastor had taken so much ground; nothing was beneath him. He could be interrupted; he would always take the time to speak life into people as he spoke into my father that day. I hoped that the seeds planted from my pastor's words would take deep root in my father's heart.

The rest of the vacation was incredible! I was completely off from work and got to spend quality time with my family. We went to cookouts with my neighbors and church friends. We went to long dinners, took walks, and watched tons of movies. It was such a relaxing time, the way things should be. I truly experienced the miraculous hand of God, as I had never seen a vacation go so smoothly, but this was God showing me how He intended families to operate and commune with one another. This was the hope of what I could have and what I should have.

I continued to grow stronger and stronger in my faith, ministering in the gifts of the Spirit and speaking and seeing miraculous signs and wonders in my workplace and encounters in and out of church. I became an unstoppable force, and my family was now fully on board.

I looked forward to talking with them, I looked forward to visiting them, and they even tremendously blessed me financially.

Part 3

The Wound Care Kit

Praise
Prayer
People
&
the
Bible

Chapter 8

The Wound Care Kit: Praise

Now that we understand what unaddressed wounds look like and how wounds have to be addressed, we need what we like to call in the nursing world a wound care kit. While a typical wound care kit in the natural world involves different types of bandages, analgesics, and wound care products to care for the wound, we are actually going to be taking those bandages off in the spirit.

There are a few weapons that every person needs in their wound care kit that aid in the healing process and are needed to advance the kingdom. They are a family of three Ps and a B, and when linked together are unstoppable forces. Healing is guaranteed! They are praise, prayer, people, and the Bible! You can't have one without the other; they all complement one another. We'll address the first family member: praise!

I love this one because it reminds me of the most intense phases of the healing processes for me. I felt like I was on an emotional roller coaster, dealing with feelings and emotions that had been so repressed for nearly a lifetime. When given a means to be expressed, I felt like I had no control. Part of the healing process is actually releasing that control. The control is what you have been holding on to for dear life, but when you let go, you actually find your life.

I remember going on these long runs, listening to worship music. As it played in my headphones, I would begin to cry even while I was running. As discussed before, this is a normal phase in the healing process. Tears lubricate the wound, but every day was different. Some days, I didn't realize just how salty that wound was, and on this day, I was particularly emotional. I meditated on the worship and let the tears flow like a river, and then I heard the Lord speak to me. I felt so heavy in my spirit. I felt like I was never going to get myself together, but again, I didn't have to do anything but let the process of pain take its course. I was learning that tears were a natural manifestation and a healthy coping mechanism. Just about the time I thought I would never get it together, the Holy Spirit said, "Dana, your biggest weapon is your praise, and this is your ticket out of this season."

As the lyrics of Darlene Zschech's "Victor's Crown" played in my head, something in me instantly shifted, and I made an agreement with God that no matter what I was feeling, I would worship and I would praise.

My praise and worship went to a whole new level. If Darlene Zschech could write an entire album based on her battle with cancer, I certainly could utilize the best weapon against the kingdom of darkness: praise. Worship and praise nourish the wound because it puts God in His rightful place in your life: seated and enthroned. Darlene, in the midst of her battle, writes songs with lyrics like "Every high thing must come down, every stronghold shall be broken, you wear the victor's crown, and you overcome! You overcome!" When I would run along singing these words over my situation, over my circumstances, all of a sudden, strength would come, clarity would come, and the spirit of heaviness would be exchanged for a garment of praise! In fact, I would play this song over and over; it was on repeat in my iPod playlist. Even my worship leading and my stage presence changed. I took on a whole new authority. I was living the words I was singing. I began to understand who I was in Christ, and I had the desire to take people to the places I had been!

I ended up having an opportunity to lead that song one Sunday morning. As I led, it was like standing outside of myself. I didn't recognize who I was because I had been completely transformed. I led out of my testimony, but it was no longer about me. As I looked out, just like I had done in the dream, I stood in the middle of the strongholds of the people in the congregation. I fought for them, and I fought until the breakthrough came.

I would continue to repeat this over and over. Daily, I could see myself going from glory to glory and strength to strength. God was training my hands for battle by lifting them up in worship and praise, unto Him, despite the circumstances!

Wound Care: Healing from the Inside Out

In a posture of worship, anxiety, fear, frustration, depression, and the cares of life have to leave and find their place. 2 Corinthians 10:4–5 (NKJV) describes this so well, saying, "For the weapons of our warfare are not carnal but mighty in God for pulling down strongholds, casting down arguments and every high thing that exalts itself against the knowledge of God, bringing every thought into captivity to the obedience of Christ."

Just look at David in the Bible. He illustrates it so well in the Psalms. He literally had to command his heart when it came to times of overwhelming sorrow and grief. It's amazing that he would start out with his complaints and petitions to God about what his enemies were doing to him and what he was feeling, but then he would command his soul (his feelings department) to praise God. When he did this, the sorrow and grief were lifted, and hope was restored. Psalm 42:5 (NKJV) says, "Why are you cast down, O my soul? And why are you disquieted within me? Hope in God, for I shall yet praise Him For the help of His countenance." Wow, if that doesn't stick it to the devil, I don't know what does. Maybe you, like David, are overcome with despair, but your praise will tell your soul where to go! Leave the sorrow, leave the despair, lift your hands, lift your head, and praise Him again! Then watch as the hope comes, watch as the joy comes, watch as the faith comes, and watch the circumstances shift. When those tormenting thoughts try to come your way, your praise and worship tell them where to go! They don't even have a foothold. SAY NO!

There is another story that illustrates the power of worship and praise. Watch what happens in 1 Samuel 18:6 (NKJV). King Saul had made David a commander over the men of war because everything that Saul had asked David to do, he did it, and he did it successfully. 1 Samuel 18:6 (NKJV) says, "Now it had happened as they were coming home, when David was returning from the slaughter of the Philistine, that the women had come out of all the cities of Israel, singing and dancing, to meet King Saul, with tambourines, with joy, and with musical instruments. So the women sang as they danced, and said:

'Saul has slain his thousands,
And David his ten thousands.'

"Then Saul was very angry, and the saying displeased him; and he said, 'They have ascribed to David ten thousands, and to me they have ascribed only thousands. Now what more can he have but the kingdom?' So Saul eyed David from that day forward. And it happened on the next day that the distressing spirit from God came upon Saul, and he prophesied inside the house. So David played music with his hand, as at other times; but there was a spear in Saul's hand. And Saul cast the spear, for he said, 'I will pin David to the wall!' But David escaped his presence twice.

"Now Saul was afraid of David, because the LORD was with him, but had departed from Saul. Therefore Saul removed him from his presence, and made him his captain over a thousand; and he went out and came in before the people. And David behaved wisely in all his ways, and the LORD was with him."

This story illustrates the power of praise. First, when we praise, we are telling our circumstances and our brokenness that despite the emotion and the grief that they may try to bring, we are victorious. Saul, in his jealousy and anger, was tormented by an evil spirit because he had given it access to his life. On the other hand, every time David played the harp, he escaped the spears of Saul and received favor even in Saul's state of hate.

When we have a garment of praise, the enemy, like Saul, can try to hurl spheres, but like David, we will escape them. Worship and praise are a sign of victory before the battle even ends. We are showing God that this is our stance in whatever circumstances we find ourselves in and demonstrate our belief that the battle has already been won!

Later on in 1 Samuel 19:8 (NKJV), it says that "And there was war again; and David went out and fought with the Philistines, and struck them with a mighty blow, and they fled from him. Now the distressing spirit from the LORD came upon Saul as he sat in his house with his spear in his hand. And David was playing music with his hand. Then Saul sought to pin David to the wall with the spear, but he slipped away from Saul's presence; and he drove the spear into the wall. So David fled and escaped that night."

You can see the outcome of two different choices. If we worship ourselves by making idols of our circumstances and falling prey to them, we become tormented and, in return, torment others. As previously described, unaddressed wounds infecting us will find a way to infect others. Hurt people hurt people. Shame turns to blame.

Or we can make the choices that David made. Despite sorrow and grief, we can command our souls that we will praise God! We can choose to make a declaration with our lips and hearts! We can lead the horses to battle, let the Lord get the victory, and let our praise and worship do the talking.

Worship is a sign of surrender. We put God in a seated place in our life. We put him back in control. We allow him to be the navigator while we sit quietly in the passenger seat! It quickens the healing. It allows the healing hands of God to go to work, softening the soils of our hearts, sloughing away the scab of brokenness and darkness, and exposing it to the light of God's love and truth. In worship, our hearts are positioned toward the answer: the unfailing love and promises of our all-powerful Savior!

Chapter 9

The Wound Care Kit: Prayer

While praise is one of the greatest weapons we have against the enemy, prayer is a close runner-up. This is the second member of the wound care kit: family. Worship puts God in His rightful place and positions our hearts toward God, but prayer is the engine room that ignites faith.

Isaiah 55:6 (NKJV) says, "Seek the Lord while he may be found. Call upon him when he is near."

Where is the Lord found? The Lord is found in our place of dependence. He is found in our brokenness and in our weakness. He is found in the place of struggle and in the unknown. If we were in perfect condition, we wouldn't need Him to fix us. If our flesh weren't weak, we wouldn't need the strength of His Spirit. God doesn't need fixed people; He wants to fix broken people. If you think you are a mess, you are in perfect condition to fix. Your brokenness was never meant to be just for you; it was meant to help someone else! Jesus was beaten and bruised not for Him but for us!

Prayer precedes breakthrough, healing, and restoration. Prayer is the engine room where the kingdom of God is established on earth. It is not just about the act of praying that brings about your breakthrough; it is how you pray.

I learned very quickly in the healing process that I would have to carve out time to pray. The most effective focused time of prayer for me was and still is the first part of the day. I prayed early in the morning before I started to think thoughts that would overwhelm me. I prayed before the busyness and cares of life came to distract me. I decided that God would get first place.

Jesus Himself often withdrew to pray. Even in his sinless state, he still had to deal with his human flesh praying in Luke 22:42 (NKJV), "Father if it is Your will, take this cup away from me; nevertheless not My will, but Yours be done."

Because He was familiar with the desires of the flesh, the inner struggles of the mind and soul, He urged his disciples in Luke 22:46 (NKJV), saying, "Rise and pray, lest you enter into temptation." If the Savior of the world felt that prayer was important to start the day, then perhaps it just might be effective for breakthrough.

I liken starting the day off in worship, prayer, and the Word of God to tithing the first part of day. It is giving God your surrender, your innermost. It aligns you to His thoughts and His ways.

But God doesn't just want us to pray passive prayers; He wants us to pray effectively. James 5:16 (NKJV) says, "The effective, fervent prayer of a righteous man available much." We have to know how to pray and how to pray effectively.

God taught me how to pray effectively in this season. I learned about the different postures of prayer and truly began to hear God's still small voice more and more. I began to gain wisdom, knowledge, understanding, and walk in truth.

One of the most important things I learned about prayer is that we have to take the time to wait on God. I had heard Pastor Phil Pringle, founder of the C3 churches worldwide, discuss this in many of his sermons and lectures in Bible College. He talked about how he would sometimes wait on God for minutes, hours, and even days. I began to adopt this as part of my prayer life. I would wait on God during the first part of the day. I would utter nothing from my lips and I would let God get the first words for the day. Often I would put on a worship song, meditate on the lyrics, fix my eyes on God, and think about His marvelous works and His awestruck wonder. Truthfully, most of the time, I would never hear anything specific. But when I went to pray and minister to someone, I would have prophetic words for them. I would have a greater level of wisdom to solve problems. I would have strategy for the things I had been assigned to do in that season. When the enemy tried to come in, it was like I could easily recite the promises of God and what He said about me. I believe that even though I didn't hear from God directly during that morning prayer time while I was waiting on Him, thinking it was all about focusing on Him, He was actually speaking His thoughts toward me. Before I could start wrestling with my own thoughts and my own ways, the Holy Spirit was actually interceding on my behalf, shutting down the power of the kingdom of darkness. The more I waited on God, the more I was strengthened. The more I was strengthened, the lighter I felt in the process, recognizing I was in Christ and receiving the authority that comes with being in Christ.

So first I waited, and then I moved on to take at least five minutes to pray in the Spirit. Some people have never been taught about having a personal prayer language, but I was thankful to go to a church that operated in not just the fruits of the Spirit but also the gifts of the Spirit. I was taught that when I prayed in my own heavenly language, I was praying the perfect will of God. I was bypassing my mind and my thoughts. The Holy Spirit was edifying me, building me up, and speaking on my behalf. It is this type of prayer that breaks the chains of darkness, sets captives free, and cancels every assignment and stronghold the enemy tries to bring. I recognized I could get much more accomplished praying in the Spirit than trying to pray with my own words. I also recognized that when I did pray out loud, either in my personal time or corporately in front of others at prayer meetings, staff meetings, or connect groups, my prayers took on a whole new level of authority. As I would pray, the Word of God would flow out of my mouth. I would pray prophetically, and my prayers brought a level of breakthrough to the atmosphere. Praying wasn't something I was afraid to do; it wasn't a struggle for me. The more I prayed in the Spirit, the more I enjoyed praying, loving every opportunity to pray for myself and other people!

The one thing we often forget about prayer is to pray from a place of thankfulness. The Word of God says in Philippians 4:6 (NKJV), "Be anxious for nothing, but in everything by prayer and supplication, with thanksgiving, let your requests be made known to God." We have to remember to thank God for the things that have already been accomplished by the finished work of the cross! Thank Him that you are healed! Thank Him that you are restored! Thank Him that His promises are true and for them coming to pass! Thank Him for what He has already accomplished in your life! Thank Him that He is your Savior and your Lord!

Take an effective prayer, combine it with an attitude of gratitude, and then add communion! Don't wait for a routine communion service in your church. You can take it right at home! When we take communion, we take the emblems representing the blood of the Lamb and His body, which was bruised and broken for us. We thank Him for what He already did; we see again the completed work of the cross and the resurrection power of the cross at work in our lives. This changes us, and when we change, our circumstances change.

Let's take a look at one of my favorite stories in the Bible that illustrates the power of effective, persistent prayer. In 1 Samuel 1 (NKJV), we find the inspirational story of Hannah. The Bible says there was a man named Elkanah who had two wives: Hannah and Peninnah. Peninnah had children, but Hannah has no children. It says that although she was barren, Elkinah actually gave her a double portion of his sacrifices and offerings each year. Each year, Peninnah would provoke Hannah about her barrenness. Eventually, this affected Hannah to the point where she constantly wept and did not eat.

The Bible says in 1 Samuel 1:10–11 (NKJV), "And she was in bitterness of soul, and prayed to the LORD and wept in anguish. Then she made a vow and said, 'O Lord of hosts, if You will indeed look on the affliction of Your maidservant and remember me, and not forget Your maidservant, but will give Your maidservant a male child, then I will give him to the LORD all the days of his life, and no razor shall come upon his head.'

"And it happened, as she continued praying before the LORD, that Eli watched her mouth. Now Hannah spoke in her heart; only her lips moved, but her voice was not heard. Therefore Eli thought she was drunk. So Eli said to her, 'How long will you be drunk? Put your wine away from you!'

"But Hannah answered and said, 'No, my lord, I am a woman of sorrowful spirit. I have drunk neither wine nor intoxicating drink, but have poured out my soul before the LORD. Do not consider your maidservant a wicked woman, for out of the abundance of my complaint and grief I have spoken until now.'

"Then Eli answered and said, 'Go in peace, and the God of Israel grant your petition which you have asked of Him.' And she said, 'Let your maidservant find favor in your sight.' So the woman went her way and ate, and her face was no longer sad."

What happened as the result of unrelenting, fervent prayer? Lo and behold, Hannah conceived because the Lord remembered the cry of her heart. She bore Elkinah a son and called him Samuel, saying in 1 Samuel 1:20 (NKJV), "Because I have asked for him from the Lord."

Further down in 1 Samuel 1:24 (NKJV), the Bible says, "Now when she had weaned him, she took him up with her, with three bulls, one ephah of flour, and a skin of wine, and brought him to the house of the Lord in Shiloh. And the child was young. Then they slaughtered a bull, and brought the child to Eli. And she said, 'O my lord! As your soul lives, my lord, I am the woman who stood by you here, praying to the Lord. For this child I prayed, and the Lord has granted me my petition, which I asked of Him. Therefore I also have lent him to the Lord; as long as he lives he shall be lent to the Lord.' So they worshiped the Lord there."

Hannah in her human nature, brokenness, and grieving heart saw the promises of the Lord fulfilled because she prayed until the breakthrough came. She didn't stop at one prayer, she didn't stop at two, but she prayed daily. She didn't care what was going on around her; she was so desperate for this miracle, for God to open up her womb. And the most beautiful thing about this story is something so essential that we need to model after this woman. Hannah gave before she saw. Hannah offered up her son and dedicated him to God before God opened her womb, before she conceived, before she bore her first son.

Hannah understood a very important principle of expectancy in prayer. When we are praying for healing, breakthrough, and praying through our state of barrenness, we, like Hannah, need to learn to build an altar for the Lord. Don't wait for the victory to build an altar before God. Pray from that victory and pray from that altar. Put your stake in the ground and tell God that this is the miracle that will come to pass and build an altar before Him.

Just listen to Hannah's victory prayer. It can be yours too if you pray and persist like she did without hiding your grievance and brokenness!

In 1 Samuel 2 (NKJV), "Hannah prayed and said, 'My heart rejoices in the Lord; My horn is exalted in the Lord. I smile at my enemies, Because I rejoice in your salvation. No one is holy like the Lord, For there is none besides You. Nor is there any rock like our God. Talk no more so very proudly; Let no arrogance come from your mouth, For the Lord is the God of knowledge; And by Him actions are weighed. The bows of the mighty men are broken, And those who stumbled along are girded with strength. Those who were full have hired themselves out for bread, And the hungry have ceased to hunger. Even the barren has borne seven.'"

What a declaration prayer! I don't believe this was the first time Hannah prayed this prayer. I believe that when the priest saw her praying in the temple and when he thought she was intoxicated, she was actually fully vigilant, fully sober, declaring this prayer over her barren womb!

God didn't just stop at Samuel, although he grew up ministering before the Lord and became quite a prophet! Hannah continued to sacrifice year after year to the Lord, and He blessed her by visiting her so that she conceived and bore three sons and two daughters! When she gave her first before, she saw the miracle: God multiplied her seed. The womb that was closed and barren was now open and ripe for harvest!

In my particular situation, I had given God everything, including my family, standing on His promises and word that He had given me about generational healing. Once I began to see one miracle, it was followed by multiple miracles, just like Hannah! This area of my life was no longer barren! In fact, my family was completely transformed. If you could have seen my previous family and my family post transformation, they would be unrecognizable. In addition, I myself was unrecognizable compared to my previous self. If I hadn't learned how to pray, I wouldn't have been strengthened to act; prayer preceded my actions.

We have to pray daily and fervently, but then we have to act. Prayer guided every decision I was making in the healing process; it required a daily surrender and submission. I wasn't just acting on my own personal circumstances; I began to truly operate in the gifts of the Spirit and began seeing the miraculous as I prayed for others.

I began to be called upon to pray for miracles and healing. I remember being an intern, and my mentor and me meeting with a woman who had a report of cancer that she didn't believe to be true. She had requested that we bind together and pray for her. This woman came to the office that day. We anointed her, prayed for a miracle, and complete healing from cancer.

As we sat in the room with her, we began to hear her story and her background. She said that she had been going to a church down the road and that she had driven by our church many times. One of the times she had been driving, she felt she needed to stop and go in. When she entered the doors of our church, she encountered the presence of God, and she knew she had to leave the church that she had been going to for years because this was now her home. I found out that she was actually one of my coworkers in the same health-care system as me. She knew all the medical facts, but she believed the Word of God had the last say, and that by his stripes, she was healed.

She was scheduled for a double mastectomy but believed that when the results came back, they would be negative. She asked us to agree with her. We all began praying in the Spirit and with authority. As we all prayed individually for her, we felt the tangible presence of God fill the room. The Holy Spirit began to speak through us prophetically. We were making a declaration that all cancer cells were leaving and spoke to the physiologic processes at the cellular level. She was healed in Jesus's name!

As we finished praying, she declared, "I know that I know that I have been healed today," with tears streaming down her face. A few weeks later, we received a report that indeed she was healed. She did have the surgery, but when they sent the tissue specimens, they came back negative without a trace of cancer. The doctors were in a state of shock, saying, "I don't know what to tell you. We have never seen this before. There is not a trace of cancer!" That beautiful woman is alive and serving in our church today with a huge smile on her face. Every follow-up appointment just gets even better and better; there is still not a single sign of cancer! That is the power of praying effectively in the Spirit. Heaven can't agree with cancer, so why should we?

A few months later, I was called on to pray for a woman in her early forties who had been sent home on hospice. Two women from my women's prayer group knew that I had been praying for healing in the hospital and in our church community, so they sought me out and asked if I would come pray for her. This woman had recently come back to her faith, and something inside of her did not agree that there was nothing the doctors could do. She had two small children and did not believe they would be left motherless. Her mother, who was new to our church, had been taking care of her for some time, but now the condition of her daughter had grown so desperate, she needed a miracle.

Now these type of miracles definitely do not require passive "if it's God's will" prayers. When we pray for these things, we have to know the authority we carry. There cannot be a margin of doubt. In fact, you have to approach these types of prayer with 100 percent faith.

In Mark 9:17–29 (NKJV), the Bible says, "Then one of the crowd answered and said, 'Teacher, I brought You my son, who has a mute spirit. And wherever it seizes him, it throws him down; he foams at the mouth, gnashes his teeth, and becomes rigid. So I spoke to Your disciples, that they should cast it out, but they could not.' He answered him and said, 'O faithless generation, how long shall I be with you? How long shall I bear with you? Bring him to Me.' Then they brought him to Him. And when he saw Him, immediately the spirit convulsed him, and he fell on the ground and wallowed, foaming at the mouth. So He asked his father, 'How long has this been happening to him?'

"And he said, 'From childhood. And often he has thrown him both into the fire and into the water to destroy him. But if You can do anything, have compassion on us and help us.' Jesus said to him, 'If you can believe, all things are possible to him who believes.' Immediately the father of the child cried out and said with tears, 'Lord, I believe; help my unbelief!' When Jesus saw that the people came running together, He rebuked the unclean spirit, saying to it: 'Deaf and dumb spirit, I command you, come out of him and enter him no more!' Then the spirit cried out, convulsed him greatly, and came out of him. And he became as one dead, so that many said, 'He is dead.' But Jesus took him by the hand and lifted him up, and he arose. And when He had come into the house, His disciples asked Him privately, 'Why could we not cast it out?' So He said to them, 'This kind can come out by nothing but prayer and fasting.'"

I had to agree with this particular woman in her battle over cancer and believe with the two women who had asked me for help. I also happened to be fasting on that particular Monday morning. I went to the woman's house around noon, so I was able to prepare myself in fasting and prayer that morning. As I paced my living room in prayer, I began to see demonic strongholds over this woman's life in terms of relationships. There was discord and dysfunction between her and her mother. I saw spirits of rejection and abandonment. I saw spirits of fear and generational oppression. I began to bind and break these spirits, bringing down strongholds and every generational oppression over this family in Jesus's name. I began to break the report of cancer and cancel agreements made with death. By the time I went to pray for her, my faith was so fully charged! I was in tune with the Holy Spirit; He was in charge, and I had my game face on. There was not a single margin of doubt. There was a reason I had been sought out and called to this home. I knew that when I left, this woman would be healed of cancer and that I would be the vessel the Holy Spirit could operate through to heal her.

Before I arrived, I asked the women to get anointing oil and prepare the room with worship music. I specifically asked them to play from Darlene Zschech's album *Revealing Jesus* because she wrote this out of her own battle with cancer.

I made the half-hour trip to this home and was greeted by the two women at the door. We made our way up the stairs, and just as I requested, this album was playing and the anointing oil was there. I met the woman's mother. She seemed very haggard and anxious as she lay beside her daughter.

I found the beautiful young woman lying in her bed, lethargic. Her words were barely understandable as she had slurred speech from her state of lethargy but was able to make out a few words. I introduced myself and told her I was a nurse. I told her I was on the pastoral team at my church and had been asked to pray for her today. I explained to her what was about to take place, that the women and I would be praying in the Spirit in another language but that all she had to do was receive what God has for her, with faith, and she would be healed that day.

I asked the women to start praying in the Spirit and to bring me the anointing oil. I took the anointing oil and asked the girl to guide me to the area of greatest pain. I was expecting it to be in her spine, where the primary tumor was, but she pulled back the covers and told me her legs were in excruciating pain. Her legs were completely emaciated, as she had probably had very little nutrition and it was obvious that the cancer had made its way to her bone. I took the anointing oil and began massaging her legs and praying in the Spirit. As I began praying in the Spirit, the Lord began to give me an interpretation of how he was healing her while I was praying. In the Spirit, I could see that she was like the story of Tabitha in Acts 9:36–42 (NKJV) in the Bible. The demographics were the same. Tabitha, who had been a disciple of Christ, became sick and actually died. They laid her in an upper room and they sent Peter to the upper room where she was lying. Peter knelt down, prayed, and turned to her, saying, "Tabitha! Arise!" Tabitha opened her eyes and sat up. He took her hand, stood her up, and presented her alive to the people.

Coincidentally, this woman, who was coming back into her faith, was lying sick in an upstairs bedroom and had been sent home to die. I was called to come pray for her. Just as Peter had said, "Tabitha arise," I told this woman that the Holy Spirit was showing me that cancer cells were leaving her body and that new living cells were replacing them. The new living cells in her body were crying out in praise to God. As I said this, the woman, who had been severely lethargic, lifted her hands in worship right there in that bed and exclaimed, "I am healed, I am healed!"

What I didn't know is that while I was praying and massaging her legs, I felt heat leaving my hands and going into her body. The women who were praying with me said that when they opened their eyes and looked, they saw fire from my elbows all the way to my hands, and in that instant, they knew that God was healing this woman!

But it didn't stop there! I turned to look at her mother, and the Holy Spirit fell upon me as I was praying. I told her mom that her healing was not the only miracle that we would see that day. I began to prophesy over her as the Lord had shown me about her life. The Holy Spirit revealed to me the anxiety, the worry, the sleepless nights, and the devastation in the relationship between her and her daughter. He showed me how the spirit of death and rejection were leaving, how God was restoring their broken hearts and breaking off chains of generational oppression. I told her that I believed that God was healing them generationally and breaking off discord, dysfunction, resentment, and animosity between them. I told her that the Holy Spirit came to heal her daughter and to heal her. They were being healed so that they too could lay hands on the sick and see them recover. As tears streamed down her face, she was in total agreement, and we prayed a prayer of deliverance and healing over her. In the midst of the prayer, she grabbed the hand of her daughter and lifted it up in worship and in agreement.

As we concluded the prayer, this beautiful young woman sat up in the bed, just as in the story of Tabitha, and asked for some medication for constipation! Wow! Being a nurse, that is a completely normal request! She seemed to come completely alive and certainly had her wits about her!

We all left her home that day knowing the Lord healed her instantly. I found out two days later that this beautiful woman and her daughter had actually been able to leave the house. All her daughter wanted to do was go shopping, so that is what they did. As I checked up on her, I kept hearing reports that she was back to her normal self, dying Easter eggs with her children. Months later, the report of cancer was shattered and broken. No hospice necessary!

These were the first of a series of miracles that I was able to participate in during this time, and continue to press in, and believe for today. Don't think that just because you are going through a healing process, you can't be used to lead others in breakthrough. That is a lie from the pit of hell. In fact, Jesus went to the cross for brokenness; grace is attracted to weakness and brokenness. You have to remember that you are the minister, but the Holy Spirit is doing the work in you and through you.

I saw patients come into the hospital with given reports that nothing could be done for them. Many of them were believers! God put me on assignment in the most grim and difficult of circumstances simply because I had a gift of faith that operated with healing, miracles, and deliverance, and I believed.

For instance, I saw a patient come in with multiple organ failure that the doctors said would not make it to transplant. Yet I received a word of knowledge that the patient would get a transplant. When the family was advised to take the patient off life support, they asked me what I would do if I were them. I help families make decisions, but I am often never asked this directly. I told his wife, who was a believer, that she might think I am crazy, but her husband would get his liver. My faith was certainly tested in this situation. What if he didn't survive? What if he didn't get his liver? My only choice was to believe 100 percent without any margin of doubt.

In the weeks following, he was the sickest of any patient I had ever had in that condition, but I was going to work out that miracle to the best of my ability. There came a day where he had a small window to get transplanted, and an organ was offered. I happened to be fasting and praying for him the day he received the offer. I received a call the next day that he received his liver and that the operation was seamless; he was barely given any blood products! He had a few complications after his surgery, but the liver itself was perfect! He walked out of our ICU and is living an even better quality of life today!

When we pray coincidences happen, but when we don't, they don't. I've seen patients who come in with clots on their lungs that the doctors say will eventually block their pulmonary artery. Because they are not a candidate for blood thinners, they most likely will not survive the operation. I have also witnessed that clot dissolve supernaturally when I prayed in agreement in the Spirit with the patient and the family! I've seen these and countless other miracles in the ICU because when the doctors said they could do nothing, I was willing to do something. Just like Jesus said to his disciples, "With God, all things are possible!"

That is how we are called to pray! Participating in this type of prayer over us for our breakthrough is truly only the beginning. The real work begins after we learn how to battle in the Spirit. God wants to heal us; He wants to heal our families and loved ones. He wants His kingdom to come and His will to be done to deliver a hurting and dying world from bondage, oppression, and sickness. It can be done, but it starts with us being willing to do it.

He says in 2 Chronicles 7:14 (NKJV), "If my people who are called by My name will humble themselves, and pray and seek my face, and turn from their wicked ways, then I will hear from heaven, and will forgive their sin and heal their land."

Chapter 10

The Wound Care Kit: People

When I was in the midst of this process, my number-one most important thing was to never isolate myself from the House of God. This would have been a recipe for disaster! As we read earlier, the birth of the first wound in the Garden of Eden happened in a place of isolation. There was no one available to discover Eve's blind spots and to lead her out of harm's way. She was left vulnerable and in perfect position to be deceived by the enemy.

If we want to move forward, we have to take an assessment of the people in our lives and be discerning of the people in our lives during this season. God showed me that I needed to make some changes in the 20/80 rule—that is, the 20 percent of people that I was spending 80 percent of my time. Those people included those who were running alongside of me, those who were in leadership over me, and the people I was investing into. For the majority of my life, I was spending 80 percent of my time on 20 percent of people who didn't want help! I wasn't gaining ground; I was losing ground!

I remember prior to going through this process, I received a word in truth and love that completely described this. One of the pastors in my church, credible and always accurate with prophetic words, prayed for me one night in a Sunday night service.

While she was praying, she began to prophesy and tell me that I was running at the pace other people were walking. By this, she meant I was striving and straining, while those people around me were resting in God. I was out of breath, out of energy, exhausting all of my efforts, and not getting anywhere! I could receive this from her in absolute truth and grace because she truly loved me and wanted me to live the best possible life. She was willing to step on my toes a little to help me see past my blind spot to the things that were obstructing my view. I received that word and started taking steps in the right direction. Not only did I have to let others minister to me and build me up, but also I had to choose the right people to speak into my life.

This is very important and very strategic in the healing process! We have to have accountability. We have to know the people to call who will tell us the truth, in love, who will help us get over the obstacles, and who will not sympathize over our sin. Even now, I know whom to call when I know I don't have the strength to push myself over the line to get to the other side. It's okay to have compassion and empathy because it's part of having a relationship, but who are those people who have been placed in a position of authority over our lives? While I had amazing shepherds whom I could glean from, who were the people I could go to that would remind me of what I had already accomplished, the battles I had already won, and remind me that my mountains had already been moved?

I had a faithful, beautiful friend whom I had met before I even started going to C3 Church. I'll never forget our first encounter. She opened the door of her home, six months pregnant with her first baby, and welcomed me with the biggest smile and the most open of arms. We connected in such an incredible way. I remember telling myself, "If this church is anything like the people in this connect (growth) group, I have found my home."

Indeed, I had found my home; it started right then and there. I would drive a half hour just to go to this connect group because the people in it were so beautiful. This beautiful pastor and I were friends at first sight, and our subsequent encounters were, and still have been, very much like the first.

When I began going through this process, this beautiful friend helped me on the days I couldn't control my emotions and on the days when they almost controlled me. Even though she had a little one and had very little time to herself because of her responsibilities as a mother, she took the time to invest in me, call me, and go on walks with me. She would let me unload, let me cry, and she would always remind me of how much of a testimony walking this out was going to be. I remember one day she said something very pivotal. It was something I held on to throughout the process. It was so simple yet so profoundly true. She said, "Dana, don't try to take control, let God unravel you."

That was exactly how I had been nearly thirty years of my life! I was wound up, numb, and so in control that I was out of control! She was giving me permission to heal, to let pain take its course, and to go through the process. I just needed to be reminded to give myself that permission.

There were times when it took everything I had to show up for baby showers, church events, and other social gatherings. I could barely pull it together, but my amazing friend was always there. She could take one look at me and know I was completely undone, yet even still, she would let me know, "I know it's hard, Dana, but you really are going to be okay. I'm so proud of you for showing up when I know you don't feel up to it." Her love and empathy were something I couldn't put a price tag on; she was handpicked to help guide me and to always show me how far I had come. When I came out on the other side, she was the one who would also say, "Wow, Dana, you are not even recognizable compared to your previous self. You are not even the same woman who walked into this church. Your life has been completely transformed, and it inspires so many other people!"

God gave me wisdom in that season to know whom to go to. I would have never survived without the leaders He placed in my life. I made it to the other side because the people running alongside of me didn't sympathize with my wounds, didn't just give me a pat on the back, and didn't send me on my way. They tarried with me, they prayed with me, they lifted my head up out of the miry clay, and they set my feet back firmly on the ground. They gave me the grace to have a few bad days but reminded me that I had the grace not to stay where I was.

Proverbs 27:6 (NKJV) says, "Faithful are the wounds of a friend, But the kisses of an enemy are deceitful." Further down in Proverbs 27:9 (NKJV), it says, "Ointment and perfume delight the heart, And the sweetness of a man's friend gives delight by hearty counsel. Do not forsake you own friend."

We need to know the people who are not just for what we do but are actually for us. They mourn when we mourn and rejoice when we rejoice! They are not afraid to bring correction even though they know it will cause a sting; their motivation is always love!

Wound Care: Healing from the Inside Out

The people speaking into our lives, whether friends or leaders, should be Christians because they need to have the love of Christ on the inside of them, the wisdom that comes from an intimate relationship with him, and spending time in his Word. These need to be people we feel safe with to be transparent and to be ourselves. We don't need to put on the mask and we don't need to put on the facade! We've already spent so much of our life doing that; we're taking the masks off, not to put them back on. We're getting healed so we can get real. The *real* people God places in our life will have the ability to speak into this process. Their words will carry authority, weight, and conviction because they wouldn't be leaders in our lives if they hadn't endured the process of pain themselves. We must all go through it; it really is supposed to be a natural course.

The other thing that we can't forsake, just as we did not forsake praying and ministering to other people, is leading people. Leaders are often deceived, thinking they have to have it all together to lead, but that is a complete lie. Leaders can lead because they take others to a place that they have already been. Often the people you are called to lead will need to glean from your experience. You have leadership over you and people running alongside of you, but never are you to negate the people you are called to lead.

I was able to disciple and minister to so many people in my workplace, in pastoral care, and on the teams I was serving at church because they knew I could handle these tough situations with grace. There was a level of credibility that I had when they would come to me for counsel because I had experienced a few things by that point and had raised the level of transparency in my life. It's amazing! People actually relate so much more to transparency than a facade because they feel safe enough to expose their struggles and ask for help!

This was very present even in my connect group. Someone in my connect group was going through the same thing with her family, but this was years after she had been married and had grown children. I remember being on the ministry team at a women's ministry meeting, and the woman from my connect group approached me to pray for her. The closer she approached, the more she began to shake and tremble, saying, "Dana, you know, you know." She would go on to describe what she had been experiencing: the uncontrolled emotions, the toxic messages she had been receiving, and the first time she was attempting to set boundaries. She felt she didn't have the strength. This completely mimicked my situation!

Since I was in the midst of coming out on the other side, I had authority to pray for her, give her words of wisdom, and walk it out with her. She went through the process with the help of her church family, and we saw her come out on the other side. She saw much breakthrough and restoration in her family.

What if I had decided that I was too broken to minister to the people God was placing in my care? There would have been a lot of people still lying in a pit of deception, victimized by fear, guilt, and shame. It was beautiful to see that the same grace that helped me get through the healing process was the same grace that God gave me to use to minister. The wound was not as salty now, but just a little bruised.

She was one of many people that I began to minister to during that time. My vision had become so clear that it was easy to see the root issues. I had the wisdom to address it as the Holy Spirit addressed it with me. When I was faithful with each person He sent to me to shepherd in the area of inner healing, He gave me responsibility for more. I would lead my patients through deliverance and healing in the hospital on a weekly basis. I would disciple and help women on my teams and in my connect group who faced some of the same issues. I could now lead from the place that God had led me.

I would be amazed at the same patterns of generational oppression that emerged in people's lives. No matter what situation these demonic strongholds of guilt, shame, condemnation, and religion appeared in, they would all behave and manifest the same. I could easily walk people through the steps they needed to take as well as warn them of what to expect in the process. They were not greatly surprised when these circumstances arose, as they were trying to overcome. They would communicate with me step by step for guidance and support; they too came out on the other side!

Your biggest battles are the next person's breakthrough, so while you are being led and shepherded, while you are running alongside of other people and taking ground, you are called to help lift others up! We need people! We were created to be in relationship with them and to be a part of the solution. We have to remember that all three of these categories of people are equally as important but serve different purposes.

Healing is about the people that are in your world, so we have to ask God to strengthen our 20/80 rule, especially during this time. We don't want to be led astray or lead others astray. Maybe we need to ask God today who those people are and let go of those relationships that are not helping

Wound Care: Healing from the Inside Out

us, distracting us, and sucking the wound dry, instead of lubricating it with grace and love. For me, in this particular season, to break off the toxic relationships in my family to sever the cord of dysfunction. Perhaps, for you, it is a significant other or a friend you spend a lot of your time with who speaks death, toxicity, and dysfunction versus life-giving words that transform you and build you up.

People are one of the basic components of our wound care kit for healing. Allow the Holy Spirit to point those people out to you. Ask him for divine appointments. Ask him for wisdom and discernment but do the work of building those healthy relationships. It seems so easy to isolate and wallow in our emotions, but those are numbing agents. We aren't being awakened to become numb again, so we choose our 20/80 wisely. We know that it's okay to receive from them; God placed them there for that reason!

Chapter 11

The Wound Care Kit: Bible

There is nothing that can take the place of the Word of God. This is one of the most important resources in the wound care kit. The Word of God shifts the mind, it changes the heart, it makes the unseen seen, it brings visions and dreams to reality, it restores, it encourages, and it builds strength. In fact, every time we read the Word of God, we apply Jesus to our situation, aiding our healing process.

John 1:1–5 (NKJV) says, "In the beginning was the Word, and the Word was with God, and the Word was God. He was in the beginning with God. All things were made through Him, and without Him nothing was made that was made. In Him was life, and the life was the light of men. And the light shines in the darkness, and the darkness did not comprehend it."

Further down in John 1:14 (NKJV), it says, "And the Word became flesh and dwelt among us, and we beheld His glory, the glory as of the only begotten of the Father, full of grace and truth."

Jesus ascended from a seated throne in heaven to walk this earth to be a human handbook and help us unlock the keys of heaven over our lives.

Nothing quickens the healing process like being rooted in the Word of God. We have to read and meditate on it in the morning and in the evening, fill our cars with podcasts, and find ourselves in the House of God every time the doors are open. We have to continuously be exposed to the Word of God and the transforming power of the resurrection of Jesus Christ.

The Word of God changes the way we think; it shifts paradigms and it changes mind-sets. When we shift our mind-set, the Word travels down and shifts our heart. The Word of God is a living, breathing life force. It is the same today, yesterday, and forever. The more we read it, listen to it, and meditate upon it, the more it will yield life more abundantly.

When we want our wounds of shame, guilt, condemnation, and pain to heal from the inside out, we must nourish and water the things that bring life: the Word of God.

Hebrews 4:12 (NKJV) says, "For the Word of God is living and powerful, and sharper than any two-edged sword, piercing even to the division of soul and spirit, and of joints and marrow, and is a discerner of the thoughts and intent of the heart."

Hebrews 4:12 (MSG) says, "His powerful word is sharp as a surgeon's scalpel cutting through everything, whether doubt or defense, laying us open to listen and obey. Nothing and no one is impervious to God's Word. We can't get away from it-no matter what."

Yes, this goes for the wounded, the sick, the tormented, the oppressed, the fearful, the anxious, and the rejected. It pierces through unforgiveness, brokenness, uncertainty, and grief. It binds to every part of the wound and is the salve we need for healing!

When we are tormented in our minds, when we have poverty-stricken thoughts, and when we are in a victimized place, we can simply begin to pray and speak the Word of God that we have read and heard. We speak his Word that was there before the foundations of the heavens and earth were spoken into existence!

Let me challenge us not to compartmentalize praise, prayer, and the Word of God! They are meant to be used together in perfect harmony. In fact, the Word of God is a perfect template for prayer when we don't know what to pray. This is another reason that speaking in our heavenly language unlocks heaven because we are praying and speaking the Word of God. We are speaking Jesus, the perfect will of God, and we are not doing this as a separate entity. We are joining the power of all of those forces working in and through our lives!

Again, I would encourage us to start off praying and meditating on the Word of God in the first part of the day before the thoughts begin to flood our minds, before the expectations of the day begin to weigh heavily on our minds, and before anything else gets to speak into our lives. Let God and His Word get the first say!

This keeps us on the offense, and we are in control of our thoughts, our emotions, what goes in our heart, and what comes out of our mouth. The Word of God is an attitude adjuster, a behavior modifier, a game changer, and it transforms us from the inside out.

Don't know how to begin?

The first step is to set an alarm if necessary, take an extra thirty minutes to spend time with God, and lean into Him. As a registered nurse, I have long twelve-hour shifts, so this took getting up at four o'clock in the morning and getting my Word on! We may have to adapt our schedules and be willing to be a little inconvenienced. Think you don't have the discipline or the energy? Yes, maybe at first, but once you start to see how revitalizing the Word of God is, once you get into the habit of making it your first, you won't be able to live without this ritual!

Practically, let's be real: if you need to set up your coffeepot, then do it! I always have my coffeepot set up, grab my Bible and notebook, throw some worship music on, and pray in my heavenly language, while it is brewing. I pour my cup and start reading! I can ingest the Word of God, but coffee (or whatever works for you) definitely helps me focus so that I can absorb and retain its nutrients!

Praising and praying in my heavenly language always helps remove the cobwebs and clean the filters so that the Word of God can be read on a clean slate! It is like getting completely empty and open so that I can get filled up again!

The Word of God brings the darkness to light; it brings clarity, it reorganizes disorganized thinking, it settles anxious or fearful emotions, it replaces fear with faith, and it brings every misaligned heart condition into alignment.

Have your journal ready and begin to write down the things that stick out to you. Look at passages of scripture in different versions, do word searches, and study the Word of God! Sometimes, this may take a few minutes. If you have the time and don't have to rush off to work, let it take hours. Let God take you on a journey each day.

I remember praying to God that I wanted a meditation, a revelation, or both, each day, and with my journal, he helped me do that. Bible reading plans are great for keeping us on course and helping us adopt ways in which we can study the Word of God. If you keep a journal, you can go back and read it maybe the next day or even days, weeks, and months later. You can see what God was speaking to you, and how He gave you strategy to deal with whatever you were facing at the particular point in time. In addition, you will see Him answering your prayers by reminding you of His promises in His Word; you will begin to see the fulfillment of His promises!

If the Holy Spirit prompts you, stop and pray. Remember, we don't need to compartmentalize the Word of God, prayer, and praise! We can do it all at once! When you hear Him speaking, speak back to Him, give Him a return demonstration of what He has just spoken to you, watch that word take root, and begin to work through your life.

When we speak the Word of God, we speak those things that aren't as if they are. We bring heaven to earth, we speak things forward, and we speak things into existence. You will find that you will start speaking these things over your life on a daily basis and speaking them over others when you pray and minister. God will begin to commit His Word to your memory so that even when you go to pray in the natural, you will find yourself speaking the Word of God!

When you begin to rise early, praise, pray, read, and meditate on God's word, you will find that your language will change; you will be hungry to engage with him throughout your entire day. Dr. Phil Pringle, founder of C3 churches worldwide, said something very pivotal once in a lecture on leadership. He said your Word life must equal or exceed your level of responsibility. In other words, the greater our capacity and influence, the more we need to refresh ourselves with the Word of God.

The healing process requires a lot of output. We are shedding off the old and filling ourselves up with the new so that we can be all that God has called us to be. As the focus comes off of us, we will take more responsibility for the part that we have to play in advancing the kingdom of God. Our Word life is pivotal not only to help mend the injured wound but to take territory throughout the course of our life here on earth.

So what does applying the Word of God look like? It will look different every day to be quite honest! Where are you today? Get in the middle of God's will and stand, kneel, or sit there!

Maybe today you feel overwhelmed with anxious thoughts and the cares of life! Then read and pray Philippians 4:8 (NKJV), which says, "Finally, brethren, whatever things are true, whatever things are noble, whatever things are just, whatever things are pure, whatever things are lovely, whatever things are of good report, if there is any virtue and if there is anything praiseworthy—meditate on these things."

Then meditate and pray Philippians 4:6 (NKJV), "Be anxious for nothing, but in everything by prayer and supplication, with thanksgiving, let your requests be made known to God and the peace of God; which surpasses all understanding, will guard your hearts and minds through Jesus Christ."

This illustrates the importance of waking up, turning on some praise and worship, waiting on God, and focusing on Him first. Speak this scripture out until his peace comes, until joy returns, and the clarity of mind comes! Think about the things that have already taken place, the breakthrough you have already received, and remember that you are no longer a slave to sin but alive in Christ. You have put away the former self and are now are a new creation in Christ. Your mind is being renewed as you speak! Giving thanks to God for what he has already done is one of the greatest things you can do to aid and expedite the healing process! Again, it's all about applying the resurrection power of the blood of Jesus Christ working in and through you! It's easy to thank God in the good times when everything is going our way, when we have understanding, and when things seem to be flowing seamlessly, but in the middle of trials, grieving, and process, it requires more. Furthermore, praying and speaking the Word of God when you are downcast replaces your weakness with his strength. It makes impossible things possible and it moves mountains.

Listen to the words of King David in Psalms 29 (NKJV) when he was going through a trial. He says, "Give unto the Lord, O you mighty ones, Give unto the Lord glory and strength. Give unto the Lord the glory due to His name; Worship the Lord in the beauty of holiness. The voice of the Lord is over the waters; The God of glory thunders; The Lord is over many waters, the Voice of the Lord is powerful; The voice of the Lord is full of majesty. The voice of the Lord breaks the cedars, Yes, the Lord splinters the cedars of Lebanon. He makes them also skip like a calf, Lebanon and Sirion like a young wild ox. The voice of the Lord divides the flames of fire. The voice of the Lord shakes the wilderness; The Lord shakes the Wilderness of Kadesh. The voice of the Lord makes the deer give birth, And strips the forest bare; And in His temple everyone says, 'Glory!' The Lord sat enthroned at the Flood, And the Lord sits as King forever. The Lord will give strength to his people; the Lord will bless his people with peace."

David offered this in the middle of war, in the middle of a season of injustice, when his heart was wounded. Even in the midst of grim circumstances, he exclaimed that there is no flood, no fire, and no wind that the Word of God cannot overcome! The Word of God is not of the circumstance but in the circumstance! When sorrow comes like a flood, the Word of God is over that sorrow. When you feel that you are in a wilderness, when everything around you seems barren, when you can't see yourself emerging out of the trial, the Word of God is the voice in the wilderness. His voice speaks to the dry, thirsty parts of your wilderness and brings them back to life. When the winds and cares of life try to overpower you, the voice of God that is heard in his Word commands the winds to cease, thus returning rest and peace again.

Maybe you are in the midst of your grieving and you need assurance and safety.

Speak and pray Psalm 91 (NKJV): "He who dwells in the secret place of the Most High Shall abide under the shadow of the Almighty. I will say of the Lord, 'He is my refuge and my fortress; My God, in Him I will trust.'"

As you find yourself nestled in His wings, leaning into Him to find safety, see Him protecting you and delivering you from the snare of the enemy. See yourself taking refuge in His wings and see His protection as you read and further meditate on His Word.

Psalm 91:3 (NKJV) says, "Surely He shall deliver you from the snare of the fowler And from the perilous pestilence. He shall cover you with His feathers, And under His wings you shall take refuge; His truth shall be your shield and buckler. You shall not be afraid of the terror by night, Nor of the arrow that flies by day, Nor of the pestilence that walks in darkness, Nor of the destruction that lays waste at noonday. A thousand may fall at your side, And ten thousand at your right hand; But it shall not come near you. Only with your eyes shall you look, And see the reward of the wicked. Because you have made the Lord, who is my refuge, Even the Most High, your dwelling place, No evil shall befall you, Nor shall any plague come near your dwelling; For he shall give his angels charge over you, To keep you in all your ways. In their hands they shall bear you up, Lest you dash your foot up against a stone. You shall tread upon the lion and the cobra, The young lion and the serpent you shall trample underfoot. Because He has set his love upon me, therefore I will deliver him; I will set him on high, because he has known My name. He shall call upon Me, and I will answer him; I will be with him in trouble; I will deliver Him and honor him. With long life I will satisfy him, and show him my salvation."

When we speak His Word, we are claiming that our dependence is on God and He is our protector. We put our stake in the ground, refusing to give the enemy a foothold. As long as we find our dwelling place in the Word of God, the enemy cannot overtake us because if God fights for us and is with us, nothing can be against us, nothing can have a stronghold over us, and nothing can overtake us, not even death!

Maybe you need to be reminded of God's peace. Simply speak and pray Isaiah 26:3 (NKJV), "You will keep him in perfect peace, Whose mind is stayed on You, Because he trusts in You."

Perhaps you need to be reminded of God's strength in your time of weakness.

Pray and meditate on Isaiah 40:31(NKJV), "But those who wait on the Lord Shall renew their strength; They shall mount up with wings like eagles, They shall run and not be weary, They shall walk and not faint."

Reflect upon Paul's word in 2 Corinthians 12:9 (NKJV), "My grace is sufficient for you, for My strength is made perfect in weakness. Therefore, most gladly I will rather boast in my infirmities, that the power of Christ may rest upon me. Therefore I take pleasure in infirmities, in reproaches, in needs, in persecutions, in distresses, for Christ's sake. For when I am weak, then I am strong."

Perhaps you need courage to take the next step of faith.

Read, pray, and meditate on Joshua 8 (NKJV). God instructs Joshua, "Do not be afraid, nor be dismayed; Take all the people of war with you, and arise, go up to Ai. See, I have given into your hand the king of Ai, his people, his city, and his land. And you shall do to Ai and its king as you did to Jericho and its king."

The Lord revealed the victory, and the finish line, to Joshua before he ever engaged in battle. His plan was his promise: he would deliver the enemy into his hand! Maybe the next step for you in this faith walk of healing is that you would remember the promises of God and speak them over your circumstances. See yourself victorious even in the midst of your battle. Everything you will ever need to win has already been given to you in the promises of God revealed in His Word!

Maybe you need to be delivered from fear.

Speak 2 Timothy 1:7 (NKJV), "For God has not given us a spirit of fear, but of power and of love and a sound mind."

Speak 1 John 4:18 (NKJV), "There is no fear in love; but perfect love casts out fear, because fear involves torment. But he who fears has not been made in perfect love."

Where fear tries to settle in the soil of your heart, speak these words. Let God's perfect love flood your heart. Remove fear so that faith can take up residence. God responds to faith; his presence is welcome in an atmosphere where fear is absent and faith abounds.

Maybe you need to remind yourself to stay faithful in this healing process when you can't see a means to the end and you have grown weary or tired.

Let Galatians 6:7–10 (NKJV) revive the areas of apathy and fatigue. "Do not be deceived, God is not mocked; for whatever a man sows, that he will also reap. For he who sows to the flesh will of the flesh reap corruption, but he who sows to the Spirit will of the Spirit reap everlasting life. And let us not grow weary while doing good, for in due season we shall reap if we don't lose heart. Therefore, as we have opportunity, let us do good to all, especially those who are in the household of faith."

Use His Word to accomplish for you what you can't do for yourself! Become dependent on God and lean into and onto Him for everything! You are part of the army leading the horses to battle, but it is actually God who gets the victory!

There are parts of this healing process when our flesh will try to overtake us and where we will want to give up. We will try to default to striving and straining in our own strength. Remember it is not by our might or our power, but by His Spirit and His Word that we can do anything! Use it wisely and use it lavishly to help you take hold of the reins and fight to the finish because it has already been finished for you!

The battles that we are fighting are bigger than us, but the Word of God is always bigger than the battle. Authority comes when we put God in His rightful place. He even tells us this in 2 Corinthians 10:3 (NKJV), "For though we walk in the flesh, we do not war according to the flesh. For the weapons of our warfare are not carnal but mighty in God for pulling down strongholds, casting down arguments and every high thing that exalts itself against the knowledge of God, bringing every thought into captivity to the obedience of Christ, and being ready to punish all disobedience when your obedience is fulfilled."

The Word of God trumps our greatest weaknesses. It binds up every area of brokenness. It mends every wound. It frees us from depression by filling us up with hope again. It brings rest to the weary soul and brings a peace that surpasses understanding. It sustains us and propels us forward. It is where we find joy unspeakable. It is where the flavor of the salt of the earth is found. It shatters the darkness by revealing truth and light. The Word of God brings authority to our lives; it opens blind eyes and it opens deaf ears. It is the redeeming power of Christ broken and bruised for us, but alive and resurrected to overcome the kingdom of darkness and bring it into the marvelous light.

People will see God's Word in us and through us even as we heal. Jesus tells his disciples in Matthew 5:14 (NKJV), "You are the light of the world. A city that is set on a hill cannot be hidden. Nor do they light a lamp and put it under a basket, but on a lamp stand, and it gives light to all who are in the house. Let your light so shine before men, that they may see your good works and glorify your Father in heaven."

People around you will recognize that you are going through the battle but you are standing in victory. The circumstances may be difficult, but they will not overtake you. The further you immerse yourself in the Word of God, the more you will see that the wind that used to shake you now feels like a breeze. The earthquakes that used to quake you feel like a bump in the road. The fire that used to burn you now just warms you up.

You will continue to climb that mountain and go from glory to glory and strength to strength. The onlookers will want to know your secret; do not keep it hidden! It is meant to be shared so that they too can be healed!

Part 4

Staying Healed

Chapter 12

Shake It Off

Once we've gone through the healing process, we now have a template for how to go through this process over and over again. Once we've removed some of the big stones, God will continue to take us through the process by addressing the small things. These are the things that seem harmless on the surface but often get in the way of where God is taking us on the journey. Since we are never completely healed until we meet Jesus face-to-face, we will continue to have obstacles, we will continue to face adversity, and we will continue to go through a process because God is a God of process.

Process brings strength, process brings the stretch, and process brings us to the next level. Let's take a look at how it works in the context of scripture.

In Acts 28 (NKJV), we see Paul writing to a church in Ephesus from a Roman prison where he was at liberty to preach the gospel. He lands safely on the island of Malta. After being a prisoner in Rome, he arrives to get his needs cared for by the kind people of that particular region. It had been cold and rainy, so the people built a fire to welcome him. As Paul was gathering sticks and laying them on the fire, a large snake crawled out because of the heat and attached itself to Paul's hand. The people of the island began to discuss this among themselves, saying that even though he escaped the sea, he would not survive this poisonous snake's grip. To their surprise, Paul shook the snake off into the fire and was not burned.

In fact, he was completely unharmed. The people had just been waiting for him to swell up from the venom of the snake and drop dead, but after they waited for what seemed like forever and saw he wasn't dead, they changed their minds!

God has given us the authority to look adversity in the face and do something about it! People who have been through the healing process know the authority in which they are given, so they can walk through the fire and not get burned. The poisonous snake, the adversity, may try to grip us, but with worship, the Word of God, and the power of authoritative prayer, we know we can shake it off!

In Luke 10:19 (NKJV), while Jesus was still with his disciples, he instructed them, saying, "Behold, I give you the authority to trample on serpents and scorpions, and over all of the power of the enemy, and nothing by shall any means harm you."

Paul understood this principle, and we are to understand this principle. There is no circumstance, no adversity, and no assignment from the enemy that can overtake you because of the resurrection power of Jesus alive and living in you. The naysayers do not approve of this kind of faith, but they have a different report when they see the miracle that follows. Applying the blood of Jesus to our circumstances gives us the ability to shake it off, just like Paul did.

Why do we have to shake off the adversity, shake off the circumstances, and fight the good fight? Because we have an assignment from God to influence and impact the people he has specifically placed in our care.

What does Paul do next? In Acts 28:7 (NKJV), Paul literally shakes off the scorpion, keeps walking, and heals someone! Paul had made his way to the estate of Publius, one of the leading citizens of that place. He had received report that Publius lay sick with a fever and dysentery. Paul laid hands on him, prayed for him, and the man was instantly healed. This opened up a can of curiosity in that particular place! When the people got wind of it, they began to come to him, and those who had diseases were healed. After Paul healed the sick, they honored him in many ways. When he departed, they provided him the necessary things that he would need in the journey.

God doesn't take us through the process of healing just for ourselves. The process is so we can go lay hands on someone else and see them healed. The process girds us up so that we won't let the unnecessary weight of life overcome the miraculous work that God wants to do in us and through us.

Sometimes, we've got to stick it to our scorpion enemies that try to hold us back. We have to shake it off, go forth, bring healing to someone, shift the atmosphere in our workplace, and be the change that we want to see in the world!

We are not conformed to what the world says about the circumstance because we don't live up to the expectations of the world. The people God has called us to are watching. They expect the circumstances to grip us, they expect the circumstances to take us out, but we have the power to shake it off.

You are no longer your former self! Your response and your reactions should now stand in contrast to who you once were! Paul was a martyr, a murderer, a prisoner, but with an encounter with Jesus, he became a minister, a life giver, a healer, and a scorpion slayer. He was an apostle, a messenger of God, faithful, loyal, and steadfast. Paul operated according to the divine purposes of God; he was consecrated and set apart. He operated according to the grace of God, receiving unmerited favor. He understood peace with God, harmony, and unity without disturbances and chaos. He understood that life was meant to be lived out of the blessing of God.

Ephesians 1:3–6 (NKJV) illustrates this by saying, "Blessed be the God and Father of our Lord Jesus Christ, who has blessed us with every spiritual blessing in the heavenly places in Christ, just as He chose us in Him before the foundation of the world, that we should be holy and without blame before Him in love, having predestined us to adoption as sons by Jesus Christ to Himself, according to the good pleasure of His will, to the praise of the glory of His grace, by which He made us accepted in the Beloved."

Paul could live blamelessly and above reproach in God's sight. He could live in love because God is love.

Chapter 13

Speak to Your Mountain

Staying healed requires you to continue to maintain a healthy Word life. As previously discussed in this book, your Word life has to meet or exceed your responsibility. Your Word life is one of the most important parts of your wound care kit as an aid to the healing process. Now we will shed light on what your Word life looks like as someone healed from the inside out, one who has faced their biggest mountain and come out on the other side!

Once I went through this major healing process, I realized that the template for how I would face new challenges was set; I understood how the process worked. Once the deeper, inner core of my heart was removed and cleansed, it was easier for the hand of God to move, for His Word to penetrate and fill.

I realized that now my Word life would determine what words I spoke over my circumstances and what I allowed to be spoken over me and my circumstances. My victim mentality was so easy to discern, and I was much more vigilant to pick up on the things I should or shouldn't allow in my life.

For example, I have been questioned a lot about why a girl like me, who is of strong faith and has so much success, is still single. Before I was healed, there was an instance where the enemy spoke very evil things to me.

I was in a Saturday night service several years ago before I went through this major healing process. I was getting all of my belongings together after spending sometime chatting with people after service. As I was grabbing my things, I heard a few of the young adult women in their early twenties talking about their wedding plans, chatting away, and jumping up and down in excitement. I was always one to celebrate with others, and on any normal occasion, even though it wasn't my season, I would celebrate others. I never wanted to be someone who was so bitter that I couldn't celebrate with someone else on their most special occasion!

On this particular night, I must have been in a bit of a vulnerable state because as they were laughing, I heard the enemy whisper, "The whole next generation will get married before you will."

I remember those words pierced the depths of my soul like a knife. Tears filled my eyes, and I choked them back. I grabbed the rest of my belongings and made a quick backstage exit to my car.

Even though I had not gone through the intense healing process, I knew, even that night, that those words were a lie, and I remember shouting, "You are a liar! Those words are not the truth!" At that point, I couldn't withstand the blows of the enemy because I hadn't quite learned to arm myself against the accusations of the enemy. Something that now takes a few seconds, minutes, or maybe a few hours took me days and weeks to overcome. I had to grieve the marks that those words left and give them completely over to Jesus. I wish I could say it happened overnight, but it was a deep struggle.

Ephesians 6:11–17 (NKJV) says, "Put on the whole armor of God, that you may be able to stand against the wiles of the devil. For we do not wrestle against flesh and blood, but against principalities, against powers, against the rulers of the darkness of this age, against spiritual hosts of wickedness in the heavenly places. Therefore take up the whole armor of God, that you may be able to withstand in the evil day, having done all, to stand. Stand therefore, having girded your waist with truth, having put on the breastplate of righteousness, and having shod your feet with the preparation of the gospel of peace, above all, taking the shield of faith with which you will be able to quench all the fiery darts of the wicked one. And take the helmet of salvation, and the sword of the Spirit, which is the Word of God."

Had I understood this scripture and stood on it, I wouldn't have allowed those words to pass through. Those words pierced my heart, and were a thorn in my flesh. They left me very weak. It took quite some time to heal from the mental anguish those words brought me and get back up on my feet.

Once I went through the healing process and utilized the Word of God as one of my biggest defense mechanisms, it helped me build immunity against the enemy. It helped me to become vigilant and watchful over my heart, over what came in, and what went out. The Word of God helped me filter and separate good from evil. It helped me become a better gardener of my heart. I was able to allow the rocky, thorny, or dead roots to be plucked out to cultivate the soil of my heart. The enemy had no means of penetrating the soil that I had used the Word of God to preserve.

Even after reading my testimony, you saw that there was a time when the healing process began that I had to face words spoken over me. Even though I was in the early stages of healing, I learned how to set boundaries, guard my heart, and take authority over the assignment the enemy was trying to set over me by speaking through my mother. Even though the words produced a familiar sting, I was quick to block the reception of them and I took authority over the operation of the spirit behind them. During that time, I had to continue to speak affirmations over myself and remind myself who I was in Christ, and I did that by standing on the Word of God!

Proverbs 4:20–23 (MSG) says, "Dear friend, listen to my words; tune your ears to my voice. Keep my message in plain view at all times. Concentrate! Learn it by heart! Those who discover these words live, really live! Body and soul, bursting with health. Keep vigilant watch over your heart, that's where life starts."

In other words, I had to learn to tune out the voices that were speaking louder than the voice of God. If it didn't speak life, I learned not to listen to it, mute, and silence it. That takes time and effort! We war against an enemy who is relentless because he knows that words have power, but the level of God's Word in us determines at which level those words will be intercepted.

Proverbs 18:21 (NKJV) says, "Death and life are in the power of the tongue." We have to be careful to diligently guard what voices are in our lives. If they are not building up, then they are tearing down. If they are not moving us forward, they are moving us backward.

Remember that 20/80 rule we talked about previously? This is where it applies. Once we learn the process, we can easily apply it because we understand our worth and our value. We understand those words can wreak havoc and cause unnecessary pain and struggle.

So what does it look like once you've gone through the healing process?

Not only are we able to readily discern the voices that should or should not be speaking, but also those fiery darts from the enemy can no longer pierce us. We are no longer girded with guilt, shame, condemnation, and fear but now are completely outfitted with the full armor of God. No weapon formed against us shall prosper!

As I'm even writing this book, I am currently having experiences where I can see the healing power of the cross operating in my life. I marvel at the progress I have made on the journey.

Recently, I had a conversation with a coworker, and still being single at this point, we were talking about the dating process. This person really blew me away by the words that he said, but this time, those words were completely disempowered before they even thought about making contact with my spirit.

As we were talking, he said, "Dana, I have worked here for three years now, and I have never seen you date anyone. There is something very wrong with this picture. What's wrong with you, Dana?"

While I was shocked because he was actually one of my Christian coworkers, I realized that he knew nothing about my situation or what I had been through. I didn't feel the need to defend myself, I wasn't taken back, and tears did not even come to my eyes.

I stood my ground and told him that everything was good in its season. God had promised this would come to pass, so I would wait patiently until the fulfillment of the promise.

I couldn't help but to stop and thank God because maybe the circumstances of the dating world had not shifted, but I had. I cried out to God, saying, "Thank you that you healed me from the inside out so that I could be a better blessing to the man you are bringing into my life. Thank you for the generational healing in my family so that this man can walk into a family that is fully restored and healed." If God had of brought me this man any sooner, it would have been a disaster for me, and for him! With God's Word, He helped me transform my mind. He helped me shed the unnecessary baggage. He opened my eyes and ears that were blind and deaf. He strengthened me in the weakest of areas. He has set me up for success.

After thanking God and spending a few minutes to glorify and worship Him, He reminded me of His promises. He reminded me of the dreams and visions that He had given me concerning my husband. He reminded me of the prophetic words that were spoken over my life concerning this matter. He reminded me of the word He gave me in Isaiah 46:11 (NKJV), promising He was bringing forth "The man who executes My counsel, indeed he had spoken it; he would also bring it to pass. He had purposed it and he will also do it."

He reminded me that I didn't have to look; I just had to be transformed. He reminded me that on the other side, He had blessing that would exceed anything I could ever ask or think. He reminded me of the battles that I wouldn't have to fight because I'm winning them daily.

God continues to answer my heart's cry with reminders of his promise; my hope is in His Word everlasting. Sometimes, if God were to honor the things we asked Him right when we asked Him, we would not be in a place to receive them. I recognize that God wants the very best for me, and He wants to set me up for success. Words can't harm me because I know who my God is, and nothing, not even human words, can separate me from His love.

Now that we have discussed how we use the Word of God as a defense against words or assignments against us, what does this look like when we speak words over others and ourselves?

One of the scriptures I pray on a daily basis is Psalms 19:14 (NKJV): "Let the words of my mouth and the meditation of my heart Be acceptable in Your sight, O Lord, my strength and my Redeemer."

Even though I am far from perfect, I am making progress. I ask God to recall things to me when I am not speaking life, truth, or speaking things forward. I am definitely tested in this area often, and I still fail miserably at times. On the other hand, I am willing to repent and change my mind on a daily basis.

You can tell a great deal about a heart condition by the words that people speak. Do our words bring life? Do they bring edification? Do they speak forward? Do they speak not only about what God has done but also what He is doing and saying to us?

I learned to use the Word of God to prophesy daily. God would give me a word about a situation, and I would prophesy that word. I would remind God of His Word and His promise, canceling everything the devil was getting ready to say. When we prophesy and speak forward the Word of God, the enemy can't get a foothold.

Healed people gain authority and begin to speak to their mountains instead of talking about them. They stop hiding from their mountains and begin running to them.

Sometimes when we haven't handled our underlying pain issues properly, we expect God to move mountains. We cry out, we pray earnestly, we ask others to pray on our behalf, but nothing happens. Our circumstances don't change, and nothing seems like it's moving. In fact, it seems to grow worse.

When we are calloused with hurt, pain, anger, and disappointment, we do not recognize the authority that we have in Christ.

The Word of God says in Mark 11:22–24 (NKJV), "So Jesus answered and said unto them, 'Have faith in God.' For assuredly, I say to you, whoever says to this mountain, 'Be removed and be cast into the sea,' and does not doubt in his heart, but believes that those things he says will be done, he will have whatever he says. Therefore I say to you, whatever things you ask when you pray, believe that you receive them, and you will also have them."

Sometimes the reason why God is not responding to prayers that ask him to move the mountain is because He has given us the power to speak to the mountain and declare it to be removed. Staying healed is exercising the power and authority we have been given to not talk about the mountain but to speak to it. Once we start speaking to the mountain, we see circumstances start to shift.

I saw this in my own life in life-and-death situations. God moved powerfully when I exercised the authority that I had in Christ and spoke his word to the mountain.

As I was undergoing the healing process, I was awakened by the Holy Spirit prompting me to call home and check on my mother in Virginia. He said, "Dana, call home, your mother is in trouble." I immediately called home, and my dad picked up the phone. He sounded very exhausted and his tone was flat. I asked him about my mother, and he apathetically said, "She hasn't moved from her chair in days. She keeps talking and nothing makes sense. She hasn't had any food or sleep for days. She just sits there—she doesn't move."

Everything in my system was screaming, "Why are you so apathetic? Why can't you help her? Have you tried to do anything?"

Then I realized that my dad was so paralyzed by fear that he was rendered helpless. He himself could not move or act.

I asked to speak to my mom. He really didn't believe I could help after what he witnessed over the past few days, but gave her the phone.

I could barely understand my mom as she picked up the phone; all she could do was weep. When she was finally able to form any kind of words, I will never forget what came next. She said, "Dana, I can't take this anymore. I am tired. I can't fight anymore. Will you come home and take care of your dad? I want to end this. I don't think he would be able to handle all of this. You wouldn't leave him alone, would you? He needs you."

That was a turning point for me. Something rose up in me. I no longer would be a victim in enabling victim mentality. I would no longer fall prey to my circumstances. I would then start speaking to my mountain! In that moment, I didn't give in and book a flight home. I didn't put myself on another rescue boat for my family. In that moment, I spoke the Word of God over both my mom and dad. I spoke to my mountain, which happened to be the spirit of death over my mom. I commanded it to leave and broke its power! I then began to prophesy over my mom, shouting with the authority I had been given, "You will not die in Jesus's name—you will live!"

I then began to pray over her. A few days later, I found out there had been a demon oppressing her for three days. In that moment, the demon left; she was able to speak again and fully function.

When my mother told me the story sometime later, she said a demon oppressed her while she was sitting in her chair. The demon was tormenting her thoughts, paralyzing her to the point where she could not move or speak. It was telling her that the tormenting would stop if she denied that Jesus Christ was her Savior. She said she told the demon, "You will have to kill me first. I will not deny Jesus!"

The Holy Spirit woke me up with a special assignment, and she was delivered from the demon oppressing her. This would not have happened if I hadn't obeyed and followed the prompting of the Holy Spirit. What would the outcome have been if I had cried with my mom, talked about her depression, and talked about her wanting her to end her life? God was able to deliver her because I chose not to console the demon but cast it out!

God turned mission impossible into possible because I spoke to the mountain, the spirit of death, and commanded it to leave in Jesus's name!

Luke 10:18–19 (NKJV) says, "And He said to them, 'I saw Satan fall like lightning from heaven. Behold, I give you the authority to trample on serpents and scorpions, and over all the power of the enemy, and nothing shall by any means hurt you.'"

Romans 8:11 (NKJV) says, "But if the Spirit of Him who raised Jesus from the dead dwells in you, He who raised Christ from the dead will also give life to your mortal bodies through His Spirit who dwells in you."

The ministry of Jesus models this in a profoundly simple way! When Jesus commanded demons to flee and sickness to go, He didn't have to use many words because He knew what authority He carried. In Mark 1:25 (NKJV), Jesus sees a man in the synagogue with an unclean spirit. He didn't even waste any time talking about the spirit or sympathizing with the man. He rebuked him, saying, "Be quiet! And come out of Him!" The demon immediately convulsed the man and came out!

Later in Mark 1:40 (NKJV), it says, "Now a leper came to him, imploring Him, kneeling down to Him and saying to Him, 'If you are willing, you can make me clean.' Then Jesus, moved with compassion, stretched out His hand and touched him, and said to him, 'I am willing, be cleansed.' As soon as He had spoken, immediately the leprosy left him, and he was cleansed."

Let's look at the story of King Hezekiah in 2 Kings 20. It says, "In those days, Hezekiah was sick and near death. And Isaiah the prophet, the son of Amoz, went to him and said to him, 'Thus says the Lord: Set your house in order, for you shall die, and not live.' Then he turned his face toward the wall and prayed to the Lord, saying, 'Remember now, O Lord, I pray, how I have walked before You in truth and with a loyal heart, and have done what was good in your sight.' And Hezekiah wept bitterly. And it happened, before Isaiah had gone out into the middle court, that the word of the Lord came to him, saying, 'Return and tell Hezekiah the leader of My people, Thus says the Lord, the God of David your father: I have heard your prayer, I have seen your tears; surely I will heal you. On the third day you shall go up to the house of the Lord. And I will add to your days fifteen years. I will deliver you and this city from the hand of the king of Assyria; and I will defend this city for My own sake, and for the sake of my servant David.' Then Isaiah said, 'Take a lump of figs.' So they took and laid it on the boil, and he recovered."

We can clearly see that Hezekiah was given the facts. He was given the diagnosis, but his words had power to trump the enemy and bring him a miracle. Hezekiah participated in his miracle by not accepting the report he was given. In his humanity, he had a moment of grieving, which is a completely healthy response, but he petitioned in prayer. Because he chose to not speak about the problem but to pray about it, God heard his cry. God saw his tears, and in His mercy, God healed him! God is a God of abundance, so He didn't just miraculously heal him; He added fifteen years to his life!

Sometimes in the circumstances, difficulties, and delayed gratification, we believe that God is not hearing our prayers. We believe He is not seeing the tears and He is withholding from us. On the other hand, healed people know that these are opportunities to stand on the promises of God that have been revealed in His Word and hold on to them.

The most powerful thing that we can do in times like these is to remind God of the promises that are in His Word by repeating them back and thanking God that they are coming to pass. This speaks them forward. Sometimes God takes us through these processes simply to challenge us to ask again, believe again, and be strengthened again. In any of these situations, though it may feel like depravity, barrenness, or withholding, God is removing so that He can not only fill but also add. Let's do ourselves a favor and renew those promises daily.

This is an area where people struggle to fight the good fight because they want to see the promises fulfilled in their time and season. On the other hand, this is the time to hold on because in these moments, our unseen is a greater reality than our seen. Our delayed gratification is a setup for a series of miracles!

Do not let the circumstances of life or the delayed gratification take you out. If you're questioning why this is all happening if you took the right steps to go through the healing process, you're on the right track. It's in these times, you are the closest to your breakthrough! Recognize the circumstances but don't let them dictate the truth! God's Word is "Yes and amen," which means he does not return void on his promises. He has an assignment for your next miracle, but while you wait, anticipate your miracle with faith; it will come to pass!

How do I know that?

Isaiah 55:11 (NKJV) says, "So shall My word be that goes forth from My mouth; It shall not return to Me void, But it shall accomplish what I please, And it shall prosper in the thing for which I sent it."

Do not wither and do not faint until you see that word completed and delivered. If God can heal you once, He can heal you again. If God has done the impossible once, He can do it again. If you've gone through this process once, you can do it again because with God, all things are possible!

Chapter 14

Staying Healed Is Serving a Greater Vision

Staying healed is serving a greater vision. Every solution that you will need in your life is directly correlated to being a part of the solution. Now that God has taken you through a major healing process, He has enlarged you and equipped you to better serve others. He healed you and continues to heal you so that you can come to the end of yourself. This is where the life He designed and created uniquely for you begins. Serving helps us to reconnect to God and people. Serving helps us resubmit ourselves to the authority placed over us. This keeps us in perfect alignment; this tests the heart condition and challenges us to live beyond ourselves.

This is so important to understanding why delayed gratification is an integral part of the growth process; it is the place where we want to quit the most because we often do not see the purpose. In God's reality, this is the place we need to push the most because this is the training field for the destiny for which we have been called. This is the spiritual gym for conditioning; this is the place for strength training. God wants to see the choices you make in the secret so He can reward them openly. God wants to test your obedience so He can promote you.

Luke 16:12 (NKJV) says, "And if you have not been faithful in what is another man's, who will give you what is your own?" God will test us in the area of faithfulness because he wants to see if we can be trusted with what is another man's heart. Are we men and women after God's heart or after our own desires and pursuits?

God will always place a vision and a dream in one man's heart to be fulfilled by another. In 2 Samuel 7 (NKJV), King David has a desire to build a house for the Lord to live in, but the Lord speaks through Nathan the prophet, communicating the vision for building the house. David would not build the house itself because David was a man of war and had shed too much blood. Instead, God said that He would rise up a seed from David and he would build the house.

David's son Solomon was born halfway through his reign. In 1 Chronicles 22 (NKJV), we see King David's strong leadership in beginning to prepare the laborers and building materials for his son Solomon to use in building the temple. In 1 Chronicles 22:5 (NKJV) it says, "Now David said, 'Solomon my son is young and inexperienced, and the house to be built for the Lord must be exceedingly magnificent, famous and glorious throughout all countries. I will now make preparation for it.' So David made abundant preparation before his death."

Further down in 1 Chronicles 22:7 (NKJV), King David speaks again to Solomon, saying, "My son, as for me, it was in my mind to build a house to the name of the Lord my God; but the word of the Lord came to me, saying, 'You have shed much blood and have made great wars; you shall not build a house for My name, because you have shed much blood on the earth in My sight. Behold, a son shall be born to you, who shall be a man of rest; and I will give him rest from all his enemies all around. His name shall be Solomon, for I will give peace and quietness to Israel in his days. He shall build a house for My name, and he shall be My son, and I will be his Father; and I will establish the throne of his kingdom over Israel forever.'"

Again, King David speaks to Solomon in 1 Chronicles 22:13 (NKJV), saying, "Be strong and of good courage; do not fear or be dismayed. Indeed I have taken much trouble to prepare for the house of the Lord one hundred thousand talents of gold and one million talents of silver, and bronze and iron beyond measure, for it is so abundant. Moreover there are workmen with you in abundance: woodsmen and stonecutters, and all types of skillful men for every kind of work. Of gold and silver and bronze there is no limit, Arise and begin working, and the Lord be with you."

King David's decision-making demonstrated his faithfulness to God and stewardship of the vision God had asked him to execute to his son Solomon. Although the desire was in his heart to build a magnificent house for God, he put aside that desire to fulfill what was in God's heart. He took responsibility not just to communicate the vision to Solomon but also to release his son to fulfill the vision.

In addition, King David made a deposit into his son by preparing the workmen and building materials so his inexperienced son did not have to pick up any slack but was given everything he needed to successfully carry out the vision. There was no sense of comparison in his leadership; he took the time to mentor and guide his son. Essentially, he paved the way for Solomon to carry out the Lord's plan.

King David willfully served the vision of God's heart and reproduced himself in his son Solomon, who willfully served the vision that was in David's heart. Because of David's obedience, God built David's house and established his kingdom and throne forever. Moreover, David's name would be renowned, and God would also establish the kingdom and throne of Solomon.

Let's take a look at the faithfulness and servant hood of Abraham. I truly believe we are still walking in the blessing of his obedience.

In Genesis 13 (NKJV), it says, "Then Abram went up from Egypt, he and his wife and all that he had, and Lot with him, to the South. Abram was very rich in livestock, in silver, and in gold. And he went on his journey from the South as far as Bethel, to the place where his tent had been at the beginning, between Bethel and Ai, to the place of the altar, which he had made there at first. And there Abram called on the name of the Lord. Lot also, who went with Abram, had flocks and herds and tents. Now the land was not able to support them, that they might dwell together, for their possessions were so great that they could not dwell together. And there was strife between the herdsmen of Abram's livestock and the herdsmen of Lot's livestock. The Canaanites and the Perrizites then dwelt in the land. So Abram said to Lot, 'Please let there be no strife between you and me, and between my herdsmen and your herdsmen; for we are brethren. Is not the whole land before you? Please separate from me. If you take the left, then I will go to the right; or, if you go to the right, then I will go to the left.' And Lot lifted his eyes and saw all the plain of Jordan, that it was well watered everywhere (before the Lord destroyed Sodom and Gomorrah) like the garden of the Lord, like the land of Egypt as you go toward Zoar. Then Lot chose for himself all the plain of Jordan, and Lot journeyed east. And they separated from each other. Abram dwelt in the land of Canaan, and Lot dwelt in the cities of the plain and pitched his tent even as far as

Sodom. But the men of Sodom were exceedingly wicked and sinful against the Lord. And the Lord said to Abram, after Lot had separated from him: 'Lift up your eyes now and look from the place where you are—northward, southward, eastward, and westward; for all the land which you see I give to you and your descendants forever. And I will make your descendants as the dust of the earth; so that if a man could number the dust of the earth, then your descendants also could be numbered. Arise, walk in the land through its length and its width, for I will give it to you.'"

One man's faithfulness to serve a greater vision led to an inheritance that we are still walking in today. Look at this passage of scripture. First, Abram moved his family and *all* that he had. Abram was willing to be sent forth without clear directions. In obedience, he went from point A when he didn't know point B. He didn't have a final destination. He didn't have something set up for him and his family on the other side. He moved from the familiar to the unfamiliar on faith! God called and He said, "Yes!" God said, "Come!" and he said, "I'll go!" Abraham moved before he was promised an inheritance, but because he moved, he got an inheritance!

Serving is more about what happens in us than through us. Can we serve in an unfamiliar, uncomfortable environment? God is a rewarder of faithfulness, but can we be obedient without a guarantee of that reward? Abraham didn't even see that reward in his lifetime, but he lived his life in faith that he would see that promised fulfilled.

Abram came to a fork in the road, a point of decision. Notice that both he and Lot had a chance to look out over the Jordan. They both had the same view. Unfortunately, Lot chose for himself, and it did not go well. Not only did the cities of Sodom and Gomorrah become infected with wickedness, perversion, and evil, but also it was completely depraved. Lot was forced to flee, his family was spared, but his future sons-in-law had to pay the price when God destroyed the whole city. Abram, on the other hand, set aside his own desires and his own needs for the sake of his nephew; he even tried to rescue Lot out of his predicament! Lot's decision was based on what he could see, which required no faith at all. Abram's decision was based on what he couldn't see because faithfulness was evident in his life!

I see the faithfulness of Abraham in my pastors, and I know that God called me to San Diego to be a part of fulfilling their vision. Like Abraham, my senior pastors were asked to leave everything they had in Australia to plant a church in San Diego where they knew absolutely no one. My senior pastor had it in his heart to plant a church in Australia on the Gold Coast, but his leader, Pastor Phil Pringle, told him to pray about planting a church in San Diego. Like Abraham, they left their family, their friends, their popularity, and their comfort to come to an unknown, unfamiliar place where they would have to start over. I can imagine the Gold Coast of Australia looked much like a Jordan. Everything was set up to look like it was the perfect location. Like Abraham, my pastors decided to obey the voice of God, to not settle for a Jordan, but to move across the world and bring something to San Diego that it didn't have: a living, breathing spirit-filled church operating in the power and authority of the Holy Spirit. I can only imagine there were many costs counted and many sleepless nights as they struggled with how they would be provided for, whether they would be successful, and how stepping out would affect their children and marriage. I can imagine no one could really fathom that kind of struggle, but I'm so thankful God called, and they said, "Yes!" God said, "Go and then you will see." They went by faith and not by sight. They sacrificed their entire life to serve the greater vision of not only what was in another man's heart but also what was in God's heart. Now myself and over three thousand people and their families, communities, and coworkers are walking in that blessing. I am so grateful for pastors who were willing to turn down the Jordan and lifted their eyes from the place they were to see the provision of God and take on the assignment. I marvel daily at their sacrifice knowing I could spend the rest of my life serving the vision of my pastors and be completely fulfilled! I know the reason we have planted three out of four campuses and are increasing in number daily is because of the sacrifice effect of our pastors. They had a willingness to choose God's heart for our city even when it is wasn't the most favorable and when the weight of that choice was painful.

Matthew 16:25 (NKJV) says, "For whoever desires to save his life will lose it, but whoever loses his life for My sake will find it." Serving a vision bigger than ourselves will constantly challenge us to make decisions. Is this about me or is this about God? Am I seeking my own reward or am I seeking God's heart?

Whenever we are seeking our own gain, we are compromising the integrity and health of our hearts, and our lives follow suit. Lot's life not only took a downward slope ending in destruction, but the next generation paid the biggest price! Abram sought the heart of God by first sacrificing not just himself but his entire family. As a result, his name was changed to Abraham as he became the Father of Nations. Even in his old age, God faithfully fulfilled a dream in Abraham's heart and gave him a son! God performed the impossible in his life because he was willing to give up his rights and his entitlement. He let his dreams die and faithfully pursued the heart of God. His entire family reaped the benefit!

God will often bring you to the brink of decision when serving what is another man's because God is most interested in the condition of your heart. 1 Samuel 16:7 (NKJV) says, "For the Lord does not see as man sees; for man looks at the outward appearance, but the Lord examines the heart."

Jeremiah 17:10 (NKJV) says, "I, the Lord, search the heart, I test the mind, Even to give every man according to his ways, According to the fruit of his doings." God will test us when we struggle for rights, position, and fame because He wants to see if we can lay them down for His plans and for His purposes. Can we be faithful? Can we be loyal?

Faithfulness in serving is a litmus test for the heart. It will challenge us on every level, but this is why He designed us for the process. He wants to mold and remold. He wants to shape and reshape. He wants to refine us over and over again. This can only be done through a process of submission to another man's leadership. Perhaps the call on our lives just might be helping to fulfill the vision God has placed in another man's heart.

Recently, I was challenged and tested for the first time when it came to submission to the vision of my pastors. Even as an intern, when you are stretched beyond what you think you can stand, the vision that God had given my pastors was so much a part of me; there was absolutely no question whether I was fully submitted. But then God tested me. I passed, but barely.

I had been feeling particularly dry. I was in the Word daily and in constant prayer but felt run down physically and spiritually. I was going to church regularly (always at least a two-service-a-weekend kind of girl) but was going through the motions.

I traveled to Virginia to see my family; I was very excited to actually look forward to a trip home. It seemed that everything in my family life was finally normalizing, so a trip home would be enjoyable, not something I would need to endure.

My mom and dad had been undergoing much stress and they were both not in the best physical state, neither of them getting much sleep. I could sense some of the strain, but things seemed to still be okay. I did my normal thing. I went grocery shopping with my dad, picked up dinner, sat around the table, and caught up on life, and then we all fell asleep. The next few days would be filled with visits with friends, family gatherings, and a wedding.

I went to my best friend's house and had a blast catching up. I couldn't help but be a little envious of all the land and house they could have for half of the money this would cost in San Diego. For a moment, my heart yearned to go back to the simple way of life; things certainly seemed easier there than California. I could have so much at the tips of my fingers; I actually considered what it might be like to move back.

Surprisingly enough, I got a message from a man who I had been involved with fifteen years prior. We decided to meet up and connect at his church. I was actually really nervous, as we had quite the chemistry in the past. We met up and had a great time; we picked up right where we left off. He was more attractive than ever, and the familiarity of our friendship came back quickly. We went for brunch and caught up on our lives, reminiscing on what did or didn't come to pass. We both wanted to seize that moment for as long as we could.

We met back up one more time, and then I was off to San Diego the next day. It was definitely something that really stirred me as we talked about the possibility of dating again from a distance. My emotions were all over the place, wondering why this would happen out of nowhere. Love comes when you least expect it, right? This wouldn't have possibly happened twice! We couldn't possibly walk away from it again.

As I was getting back to San Diego, I immediately started to get calls and texts from people at church. I could already feel the struggle begin. On one hand, I was excited to share my random experience. I mean, what single girl doesn't like a little excitement? On the other hand, I knew that if it were to ever work, I would have to move home, and my mind began entertaining it.

Over the next few weeks, this man and I talked or texted each other. I enjoyed talking to him and thinking of the possibilities of maybe pursuing a relationship, but then the still small voice of God came even in the midst of my busy thoughts.

I heard God say, "Where is your loyalty?"

I knew that was God's voice because when God is trying to correct, He either asks a question or makes an extraordinary statement!

I ignored him several times, but I kept hearing Him ask that same question, "Where is your loyalty?"

As I started to think about my leaders and my church, the peace began to leave. The unsettling, sinking feeling in my stomach came, bringing me discomfort and anxiety. I got a vision of what my life would look like there. Perhaps I could have the family life I had always dreamed of and the perfect house on a perfect piece of land, but I would die spiritually. I saw simplicity and comfort, but I saw myself settling for a life I wasn't meant to live.

God didn't rescue me out of bondage and heal me from oppression just to go back to Egypt to become a slave! The life in San Diego may look different. It may be challenging and uncomfortable, but I was called to greater.

Then God challenged me again, saying, "Dana, do you want to trade what is consistently consistent for what is consistently inconsistent?"

I knew He was right. Although my family did get restored and had begun the healing process, there had been many setbacks, and things were still a bit of a roller coaster at times. I couldn't really depend on the stability of my family because there were still cyclic patterns; they were still on a different part of the journey. But what I could depend on was the family, friends, and healthy relationships I had established through my beautiful church that were not perfect but reliable, faithful, and unconditional.

As I thought about my leadership again and everything I had overcome to get to that very place, I made my decision. My loyalty was still to my pastors and the vision God had placed in their hearts. I didn't beat myself up for coming to this fork in the road. Instead, I saw it as an opportunity to reconnect with God and resubmit to leadership knowing that there must be an incredible harvest of breakthrough on the other side!

God allowed that situation to happen to test my loyalty. At first, it seemed confusing. God showed me that it had nothing to do with the guy, who would still remain a great friend, but it had everything to do with my obedience. When I made the decision, He spoke again and said, "Dana, you saw a Jordan. Keep your eyes fixed on Me and run your race. Don't look to the left or the right because you will get discouraged. Remember, it may not look the way you think it should look, but I knew your end from the beginning."

Instantly, the peace returned. I fell in love with Jesus all over again and with the vision that was in the hearts of my senior pastors and leaders. I was fully recharged and thanked God for His protection!

This experience really helped me understand that serving keeps us accountable because it keeps us humble. When we are humble, we remain teachable. As long as we walk this earth, we will never arrive. Serving a greater vision will always humble us because we have to deny ourselves. James 4:6 (NKJV) says, "God resists the proud, But gives grace to the humble." The MSG version literally says this about pride: "You're cheating on God. If all you want is your own way, flirting with the world every chance that you get, you end up enemies of God and his way. And do you suppose God doesn't care? The proverb has it that he is a 'fiercely jealous lover' And what he gives in love is far better than anything you'll find."

Further down in James 4:7 (MSG), it says, "So let God work his will in you. Yell a loud no to the Devil and watch him scamper. Say a quiet yes to God and he'll be there in no time." In other words, humility allows God to have his way with us. It allows our heart to become his heart and our ways to become his ways.

Serving allows us to get so caught up in seeing the hand of God move in others that we forget about the distractions and the things that try to take us out in our prideful state. Nothing fires me up more than seeing someone receive Jesus for the first time, someone experiencing a miracle for the first time, and seeing people's lives get radically changed. Serving knits our hearts to the heart of Jesus and helps us get a greater perspective and deeper revelation of the love and heart of God. The minute we stop serving is the minute we stop living because serving is truly what gives us our greatest purpose.

Jesus himself demonstrated this. He descended from heaven to come to this earth to set an example of the ultimate servant. Matthew 20:28 (NKJV) says, "Just as the Son of Man did not come to be served, but to serve, and to give His life a ransom for many."

If anyone had a right to entitlement, it was Jesus. He left the throne of heaven, lived a blameless life, and gave it to people who had not yet even chose Him. But He knew his purpose. In fact, hours before his death, in the brink of his decision to give His life for all mankind, He prays to His Father in John 12:27 (NKJV), saying, "Now my soul is troubled, and what shall I say? 'Father, save me from this hour?' But for this purpose I came to this hour. Father, glorify your name."

He performed miracles, signs, and wonders. He overcame every temptation from the devil. He gave up every right He had, even his right to life, to honor His Father. He didn't just serve to lead by example; He served to influence. From developing his twelve disciples to the Sermon on the Mount, His life was the perfect picture of servant hood. He gave us the greatest advice any man could ever give on servant hood in John 12:26 (NKJV), saying, "If anyone serves me, let him follow Me; and where I am, there my servant will be also. If anyone serves Me, him my Father will honor." He served and led by two very powerful words: "Follow me."

The key to staying healed is being faithful in what God is giving us today. Can we sow the seed that He has placed in our hands today? Can we serve a greater vision? Can we be faithful with what is another man's? We were given one life—what will we do with it?

I think Paul's message to the elders of the church in Ephesus in the book of Acts 20:18–24 (NKJV) sums serving up perfectly. It says, "And when they had come to him, he said to them, 'You know, from the first day that I came to Asia, in what manner I always lived among you, serving the Lord with all humility, with many tears and trials which happened to me by the plotting of the Jews; how I kept back nothing that was helpful, proclaimed it to you, and taught you publicly and from house to house, testifying to Jews, and also to Greeks, repentance toward God and faith toward our Lord Jesus Christ. And see, now I go bound in spirit to Jerusalem, not knowing the things that will happen to me there, except that the Holy Spirit testifies in every city, saying that chains and tribulations await me. But none of these things move me; nor do I count my life dear to myself, so that I may finish my race with joy, and the ministry which I received from the Lord Jesus, to testify the gospel of the grace of God.'"

Paul's journey was not absent of trials, tribulations, discouragement, and delayed gratification. He lived his life from a place of servant hood, not leaving anything undone so that he could bring glory to God! Paul understood his race, and he stayed in his lane!

Serving is God's process! We must do as Paul did and run our race with endurance but stay in our lane. We must remove the comparison because God has designed us uniquely. If we look to the right or the left, we will lose sight, get discouraged, get deceived, and get tripped up. Serving a greater vision is painful. It stretches us beyond where we think we can go, but it brings an immeasurable blessing beyond anything we can ever imagine or believe. We are blessed to be a blessing, but the greatest reward is falling in love over and over again with the blesser!

Chapter 15

Staying Healed Is Having Next-Generation Generosity

Nothing captures the heart of God more and can keep our hearts healthy, aligned, and whole than generosity. Serving and giving are generosity in action and unlock abundance in every area of our lives. My heart's cry is to always be in a position to bless others. Again, God is not concerned as much about what we do as He is about who we are. He is most concerned with the condition of our hearts.

Matthew 6:21 (NKJV) says, "For where your treasure is, there your heart will be also." The MSG version goes further to say, "Don't hoard treasure down here where it gets eaten by moths and corroded by rust or—worse!—stolen by burglars. Stockpile treasure in heaven, where it is safe from moth and rust and burglars. It's obvious, isn't it? The place where your treasure is, is the place you will most want to be, and end up being."

Obvious, isn't it? For many people, this is an incredible struggle because the love of money governs many human hearts, but for those who have gone through the healing process, it now becomes a natural inclination not to just give time but to give finances.

How do I know that? This is the area of my life that truly bears the most fruit. It comes with its challenges, but the blessing by far surpasses the sacrifice. I can't even begin to count the ways in which even at the age of thirty-two, I have been blessed beyond measure and have truly witnessed the demonstration of the miraculous. It is certainly not easy and does require faith, but a healthy heart can handle the stress! Generosity sets me up for healing and breakthrough, and it keeps me healed.

The first thing we have to do is recognize the why behind the what. We are not called to religion. We are called to relationship, so we have to recognize that generosity has to do with our relationship with God. It places us in a deeper connection with his heart. It increases vision and broadens our capacity, giving positions us for blessing others and ourselves.

Generosity is really about setting up the future of the next generation. God is a generational God; His will is for the generations to partner together. Often, however, they work against one another. We have to take the responsibility here on earth to build a legacy through our generosity so that we regenerate the next generation, not degenerate them.

I learned the concept of giving at a young age, but more from a religious action and not as a principle in which I should live. Even at five years old, I tithed my allowance, and I did it with a cheerful heart. Even though I learned to give out of legalism and religion, I am very grateful that the seed was planted at such an early age and became a habit throughout my lifetime.

I really didn't learn the principles of giving until I came to C3 Church San Diego. I had been to many churches that passed buckets, participated in miracle offerings, and the like, but I had never actually heard any messages on giving. At our church, the tithe and offering message is one of the most crucial parts of the service; it was the first time I heard the word "abundance" associated with giving. I was, and still am, deeply inspired every week by these messages! In fact, the giving message is one of my favorite parts of the service because I know it means instant breakthrough.

Giving directly correlates with a change in heart condition, and blessing supernaturally follows suit. We understand that tithing takes care of our needs, but giving above that tithe takes care of the needs of others. This is where we see the supernatural overflow of God.

Previously, we talked about God testing us, but giving is actually the one place God gives us permission to test him. Malachi 3:10–11 (NKJV) says, "'Bring all the tithes into the storehouse, That there may be food in My house, And try me now in this,' Says the Lord of hosts, 'If I will not open for you the windows of heaven And pour out for you such blessing That there will not be room enough to receive it. And I will rebuke the devourer for your sakes, So that he will not destroy the fruit of your ground,

Nor shall the vine fail to bear fruit for you in the field, Says the Lord of hosts; And all the nations will call you blessed, For you will be a delightful land, Says the Lord of hosts.'"

We can clearly see the hand of God when we come to the end of ourselves. I got this revelation immediately when I came to C3 San Diego in 2010. Tithing was always a no-brainer for me, and I never seemed to have a problem with my finances. I gave to charity and purchased meals and gifts for others, but the whole idea of giving with vision was a whole new concept.

My pastors began to talk about a giving initiative called Rise and Build. This initiative is now known as Vision Builders. As I previously discussed, my senior pastors came to San Diego with a vision to plant one church in multiple locations. Vision Builders was an annual commitment to give above the tithe so that we could help fulfill that vision.

I remember that first year, my heart was stirred, and I was so excited! I couldn't wait to release the offering and see what God would do! The first amount seemed like a reasonable sacrifice, but honestly, it was not a huge stretch. I gave willingly and generously, but deep inside, I was more caught up in the overall blessing and gain. It was actually okay to expect blessing and prosperity because God is a God of blessing and prosperity. On the other hand, I started to notice that the more I gave, the more my perspective began to shift.

I didn't just tithe and give to Vision Builders; I was able to give generously to guest speakers and sponsor youth for summer camp and both men and women for conferences. The more I gave, the more I saw the value in other people having access to the things I had access to and wanted to see them blessed the way God was blessing me. I began to see that it was my responsibility not to hold on to the blessing but to release it in other people.

Each year, I was challenged to double my commitment; and each year, God came through miraculously. The numbers did not make sense. I wasn't working overtime and I didn't have a second job, yet I was able to give nearly half of my income away.

In the second year of my increased commitment, the Holy Spirit began to speak to me, and the more I prayed, the more I began to speak with vision. I would prophecy to my family and friends that this would be the year that my student loans would be paid off, and I would become debt-free. My beautiful senior pastor who prayed over me one night confirmed this. She had no idea of the revelation that I received but said, "There is a school loan, and the Lord is showing me that this loan will be paid off this year." Every year, I would receive prophecies over financial blessing; and every year, I would see those prophecies come to fruition. Indeed, I did pay off that student loan, and I did become debt-free!

Going into Vision Builders my third year at the church, I doubled the amount again and felt the Holy Spirit put home ownership on my heart. I struggled with this for quite some time but found myself saying, "I am now debt-free—I am going to buy a home." I had to speak it before I actually believed it in my heart. Renting in San Diego where the real estate market was outrageous seemed much more comfortable. Overall, my preference was to purchase a home with my future husband when it seemed appropriate. As a single person, I did not want to take on the responsibility of a home; it was much more convenient to let a landlord deal with everything.

The Holy Spirit began to push me out of the convenient. I began the incredible pursuit with a beautiful realtor from our church. I fell in love with this incredible home that was probably a little out of my league, but I went for it anyway. Much to our surprise, when she took me to look at it on the inside, it was nothing short of a crack house! Everything would have to be ripped out; the entire place would need a complete renovation, which would cost around $100,000! Needless to say, I moved on and realized I needed something more economical for a first-time home purchase.

I was encouraged by the realtor to keep looking, but I couldn't help but feel greatly discouraged. I started to shrink back in my faith. I started thinking that I didn't hear God correctly. I started exploring other options. I even thought about renting a house with a couple from church to save up more money for the purchase. In the meantime, I continued to pray, and I couldn't let go of the inclination from the Holy Spirit that I was not to rent again. The Holy Spirit said, "You are not a renter—you are a homeowner!"

I wrestled for about a month or so, and the realtor kept contacting me, sending me tons of listings. There was a particular listing that she sent me that we had previously discussed, and I had turned it down. Then I began to read the book *Draw the Circle* by Mark Batterson. I decided that the first thing I would circle in prayer would be my next home. I prayed about my home for nearly an hour. When I finished praying, I opened up social media, and the realtor had posted the listing she had offered me. She encouraged anyone to message her if they were interested.

I knew this was confirmation, so I e-mailed her right away. She basically said that she would open it up to me, and we would go forward with the offer. This house had some complications, but I knew that this particular one was an assignment from God to purchase; to win this battle, it would take some warfare.

After four months of fasting, praying, and believing for this house, going through all the ups and downs, dealing with banks' near foreclosures, they finally accepted my offer pending a fourteen-day escrow! We literally saw the miraculous because two days prior to them accepting my offer, they had made the decision to foreclose and weren't letting us fight it at all. Not only did they accept my offer, but also they met me halfway. I walked into $20,000 of equity instantly! This was the exact amount of increase that I had pledged to Vision Builders that year! This was not a coincidence! This was a *Godcidence!* When he asks us to give a certain amount, and it sounds like a crazy figure, he has a miracle planned, but we have to set it in motion!

The fourteen-day escrow was extremely stressful, as everything had a time stamp, but I had complete favor! Paperwork was processing at lightning speed. I happened to be off of work on the days there were big crunches. All of the banks were working with me beautifully. It was amazing to see the favor of God as we pushed through!

I received my keys one beautiful November day. I remembered feeling like I would have fallen right over if someone pushed me, but the vision had come to pass! God's Word rang true, "If you build my house, I will build yours."

If we prioritize God's house, there is nothing that he won't do for us. Later, when I reflected on my home purchase, I asked God why he chose me to be a homeowner when there were so many other people who had this dream in their hearts. I was single with one income, and I was interning for my church! I certainly did not meet the demographic of a homeowner in the state of California! The Holy Spirit clearly spoke to me and said, "Dana, you bought a home because of the price tag that you were willing to put on the next generation, not at their expense."

We should see the fruit of our generosity begin in our lifetime and continue in the next generation. What are we willing to give so that future of the next generation is bright? Are we willing to step out of the way of our own desires to pave the way for them? Do they have to fall behind picking up what we were responsible for in our lifetime? Can we give them a running start so they can go even further and do even greater? I describe this type of vision as having harvest eyes—harvest eyes see into the next generation.

The more God healed me, the more I began to understand not just his works but also his ways. After that long season of going through the battles, the breakthroughs, and the victories, I took a vacation to Cabo, San Lucas, Mexico, to be still and to reflect. I was at the pool one day, reading some material that I had brought to resource myself on my vacation. Having a desire to start a business in the future, I was reading *Jesus Entrepreneur* by Laurie Beth Jones.[2] This book illustrated Jesus in the marketplace and how to use the principles he taught the disciples to help us start fruitful businesses today. In the beginning of the book, Jones talked about how the marketplace would restructure job descriptions in the future. She said that the marketplace would actually go away from a job description focus to a mission-based focus because most people felt they wanted to do something that didn't just earn a paycheck but gave them purpose. Sadly, they had done some research showing that when nearly 70 percent of people were asked what they wanted most in their life now, their response was to retire! In her book, Jones quoted, "Show me someone who can't wait to retire and I'll show you someone who hates his or her job."

As I was reflecting on giving from a place of mission, I thought about some of the books I had read discussing the importance of having a personal mission statement. The Holy Spirit spoke to me and asked, "What is your personal mission statement?"

I thought about it for a few minutes and was embarrassed to say I had no personal mission statement. I had been to seminars and meetings about entrepreneurship and marketplace ministry, but I had no personal mission statement!

The Holy Spirit graciously spoke to me later and said, "This is your mission statement. Your mission is very simple." (I knew this was the Holy Spirit because he put into five words what I would have put into five hundred.) He said, "Your mission is to always make people your greatest investment."

Those words hit me like a ton of bricks; they were so simple but profound. And then I thought about the same scripture we discussed previously in Matthew 6:21 (NKJV): "For where your treasure is there your heart will be also." If my mission was to make people my greatest

---

[2] Jones, Laurie Beth. *Jesus, Entrepreneur,* NY: MJF Books, 2001.

investment, and if the Bible said that where my treasure is, there my heart will be also, then people equal treasure.

If people equal treasure, then people get the first fruits. They get our best, not our leftovers. Why? Because John 3:16 (NKJV) says, "For God so loved the world that He gave us His only begotten Son." God gave his everything so that we can give something. What I love about the church is that we do not give according to a job description. We don't give according to the dos and don'ts of religion. We give from a place of mission knowing that treasure lies in our local mission fields, our education systems, the media, the health-care system, our neighborhoods, our communities, our workplaces, our grade schools, and our high schools and colleges.

There is only one way that the gospel can be transported to reach this generation and the generations to come: through the vehicle of the church! Through giving, we fuel that vehicle so that it doesn't sit idle but moves forward taking as many people as it can to an eternal destination!

If we give with that kind of heart, there is nothing that our Father in heaven won't do for us. The Holy Spirit spoke to me again and said, "When you make people your greatest investment, you are included in that investment." If we can cultivate a next-generation generosity in our lives, we will never have to settle for anything less than God's best.

The life God has given us to live is blessed to be the breakthrough for the next generation. God wants to perform miracles in our lives so we can be a miracle for the next generation! It takes tenacity in giving. It takes faith, but it brings a hope and an assurance that they don't have to pick up the depravity, the oppression, and the poverty mentality of this generation. We are blessed to be a blessing, to be abundant in all things, lacking nothing, to bring an offering to the next generation! We were wounded to win and to reign in this life so that the future generations can walk in victory!

Conclusion

The night I knew I had been healed was an extraordinary Tuesday night. We were at a creative leaders' night in the home of one of the beautiful couples in our church in worship. We were all in complete surrender, completely engaged, offering our whole hearts in worship and praise. I'll never forget how powerful this experience was as many of us actually saw the presence of angels in the room while we were singing together. In the middle of worship, I saw a vision of the hand of God, the great surgeon, holding my heart, and stitching it back together after a long season of being on the surgeon's table. It was then I knew He had completely healed me for the first time. The assignment for my deliverance and healing had been completed. It was His signature showing me I was fully redeemed and restored.

I went through this process of healing so that I could have a template for the processes I would continue to go through. God continues to tear down and strip away. Pain is now a natural course for me, and I'm enjoying experiencing God take me from glory to glory and strength to strength.

I am not immune to pain, disappointment, and hurt, but I do not worry about my life. I do not worry what I will eat, what I will drink, where I will live, whom I will marry, or what comes next. I can look adversity in the face. I don't just run to my mountains; I welcome them. I am no longer a slave to fear because I want to be the best version of me.

I want my life to give glory to God because of all that he has given me. I know that for whom much is given, much is required. If we want to influence, change the world and raise the next generation to do things beyond anything we could have imagined or dreamed; we have to pay the price to get set free and live from that place. The victory was already won; our greatest enemy was already defeated! We simply have to remind the devil every day and live the life we are called to live.

I leave you with a final passage of scripture in Romans 8 (MSG) where Paul is speaking to the Romans:

"With the arrival of Jesus, the Messiah, that fateful dilemma is resolved. Those who enter into Christ's being-here-for-us no longer have to live under a continuous, low-lying black cloud. A new power is in operation. The Spirit of Life, Christ, like a strong wind, has magnificently cleared the air, freeing you from a fated lifetime of brutal tyranny at the hands of sin and death.

"God went for the jugular when he sent his only Son. He didn't deal with the problem as something remote and unimportant. In his Son, Jesus, he personally took on the human condition, entered the disordered mess of struggling humanity in order to set it right once and for all. The law code, weakened as it always was by fractured human nature, could never have done that.

"The law always ended up being used as a Band-Aid on sin instead of a deep healing of it. And now what the law code asked for but we couldn't deliver is accomplished as we, instead of redoubling our own efforts, we simply embrace what the Spirit is doing in us."

Further down in Romans 8:9 (MSG), Paul goes on to further say, "But if God has taken up residence in your life, you can hardly be thinking more of yourself than of him. Anyone, of course, who has not welcomed this invisible but clearly present God, the Spirit of Christ won't know what we're talking about. But for you who welcome him, in whom he dwells—even though you still experience all the limitations of sin—you yourself experience life on God's terms.

"It stands to reason, doesn't it, that if the alive and present God who raised Jesus from the dead moves into your life, he'll do the same thing in you that he did in Jesus, bringing you alive to himself. When God lives and breathes in you, you are delivered from that dead life. With his Spirit living in you, your body will be alive as Christ's."

What a message of hope! I cannot conclude this book without an invitation to those who may not know Jesus. You now have an opportunity to welcome this Savior, Jesus, to take residence in your life. All you have to do is pray a simple prayer:

"Jesus, I receive You as my Lord and Savior. I ask that You forgive me of all of my sins and I give up my rights to hold on to guilt, shame, and condemnation. I invite You into my heart to live. Help me experience life on Your terms—the abundant life of blessing I was created to live."

May I encourage us all to stay the course, run this race, and look forward, look upward so that we can lay hold of everything that Christ has already won for us.

Remember, He personally carried our sins in His body on the cross so that we can be dead to sin and live for what is right. By His wounds, we are healed.

By His stripes, we are healed from the inside out!

Printed in the United States
By Bookmasters